Taste*of*Home

Valentine's
Day

THIS BOOK IS GIVEN TO:

WITH LOVE FROM:

TASTE OF HOME BOOKS • RDA ENTHUSIAST BRANDS, LLC • MILWAUKEE, WI

© 2021 RDA Enthusiast Brands, LLC.
1610 N. 2nd St., Suite 102,
Milwaukee, WI 53212-3906

Visit us at **tasteofhome.com** for
other Taste of Home books and
products.

ISBN: 978-1-61765-995-9
LOCC: 2020942851

Executive Editor: Mark Hagen
Senior Art Director:
Raeann Thompson
Editor: Amy Glander
Art Director: Maggie Conners
Designer: Arielle Jardine
Copy Editor: Amy Rabideau Silvers

Cover
Photographer: Grace Natoli Sheldon
Set Stylist: Melissa Franco
Food Stylist: Leah Rekau

Pictured on front cover:
Chocolate Chip Red Velvet
Whoopie Pies, p. 146
Pictured on back cover:
Berry-Beet Salad, p. 61
Soft-Hearted Hello Wreath, p. 31
Glazed Doughnut Holes, p. 23
Art with Heart Cork Craft, p. 157
Chocolate-Topped Strawberry
Cheesecake, p. 123

Printed in China.
1 3 5 7 9 10 8 6 4 2

Table of Contents

More ways to connect with us:

BRING ON THE LOVE THIS VALENTINE'S DAY

with a meal your sweetheart is sure to remember. Creating a heartfelt celebration is easy with the latest edition in our popular series of mini books—*Taste of Home Valentine's Day*. This brand-new title is Taste of Home's love letter to Feb. 14, featuring our best recipes for the most romantic day of the year: dazzling dinners, swoon-worthy desserts, indulgent homemade chocolates and candies, eye-opening breakfasts, adorable heart-shaped treats, and other recipes sure to win hearts! In addition to recipes that woo, you'll fall in love with chocolate and wine pairing ideas, easy crafts, clever party ideas and a bonus Galentine's Day section for creating the perfect party for your gal pals. Filled with over 100 decadent and heavenly recipes, this keepsake collection is one you'll treasure for years to come.

Valentine's Day Menus

TAKE THE GUESSWORK OUT OF MENU PLANNING WITH THESE EASY MEAL IDEAS.

ROMANTIC DINNER FOR TWO
Serves 2

Beef Filets with
Portobello Sauce, 113

Berry-Beet
Salad, 61

Chocolate-Dipped
Strawberries, 25

Champagne
Cocktail, 33

FAMILY VALENTINE PARTY
Serves 4-6

Garlic Clove
Chicken, 109

Twice-Baked
Red Potatoes, 73

Molded Strawberry
Salad, 65

Favorite Coconut
Cake, 131

CASUAL YET COZY
Serves 4-6

Heart-Topped Chicken
Potpie Soup, 57

Buttermilk
Angel Biscuits, 80

Peanut Butter
Cutout Cookies, 137

Chocolate-Covered
Pretzels, 179

GALENTINE'S DAY BRUNCH
Serves 6-8

Buttermilk Pecan
Waffles, 197

Honey Poppy Seed
Fruit Salad, 190

Sugared Doughnut
Holes, 193

Sparkling Coconut
Grape Juice, 198

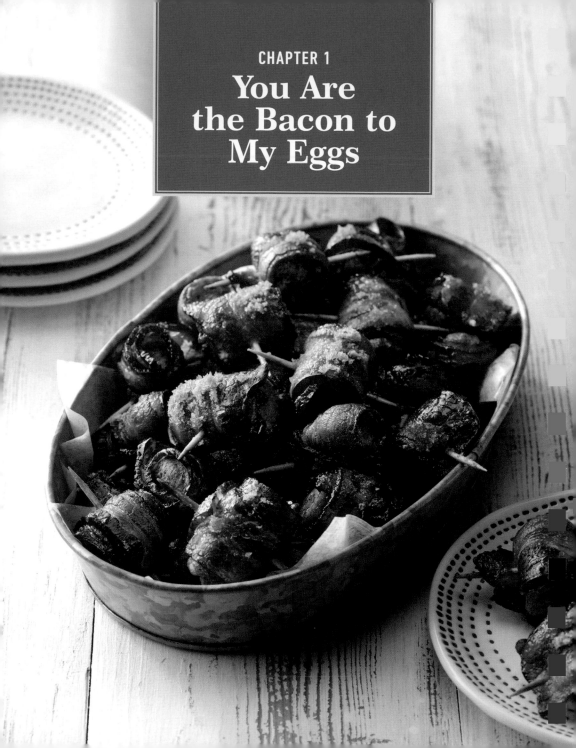

CHAPTER 1
You Are the Bacon to My Eggs

Sausage Bacon Bites

These tasty morsels are perfect with almost any egg dish or as finger foods that party guests can just pop into their mouths.

—Pat Waymire, Yellow Springs, OH

PREP: 20 MIN. + CHILLING • **BAKE:** 35 MIN. • **MAKES:** ABOUT 3½ DOZEN

¾ lb. sliced bacon
2 pkg. (8 oz. each) frozen fully cooked breakfast sausage links, thawed
½ cup plus 2 Tbsp. packed brown sugar, divided

1. Preheat oven to 350°. Cut bacon strips widthwise in half; cut sausage links in half. Wrap a piece of bacon around each piece of sausage. Place ½ cup brown sugar in a shallow bowl; roll sausages in sugar. Secure each with a toothpick. Place in a foil-lined 15x10x1-in. baking pan. Cover and refrigerate 4 hours or overnight.

2. Sprinkle with 1 Tbsp. brown sugar. Bake until bacon is crisp, 35-40 minutes, turning once. Sprinkle with remaining brown sugar.

1 PIECE: 51 cal., 4g fat (1g sat. fat), 6mg chol., 100mg sod., 4g carb. (4g sugars, 0 fiber), 2g pro.

READER REVIEW

"This made a great last-minute after-school snack for a house unexpectedly filled with tween boys! Obviously, I didn't wait 4 hours before baking. But I was voted best mom that afternoon!"

—MAMAKNOWSBEST, TASTEOFHOME.COM

Cheese & Fresh Herb Quiche

With herbs from the garden to use, I created a quiche with basil, parsley and dill along with feta, Swiss, Gruyere and mozzarella. Goat cheese is also yummy.

—*Sonya Labbe, West Hollywood, CA*

PREP: 15 MIN. • **BAKE:** 25 MIN. + STANDING • **MAKES:** 6 SERVINGS

1 **sheet refrigerated pie crust**
½ **cup shredded part-skim mozzarella cheese**
½ **cup shredded Swiss cheese**
½ **cup shredded Gruyere or additional Swiss cheese**
½ **cup crumbled feta cheese**
5 **large eggs**
1 **cup half-and-half cream**
1 **Tbsp. minced fresh basil**
1 **Tbsp. minced fresh parsley**
2 **tsp. minced fresh dill**

1. Preheat oven to 400°. Unroll crust into a 9-in. pie plate; flute edge. Sprinkle cheeses into crust. In a large bowl, whisk eggs and cream until blended. Stir in herbs; pour over top.

2. Bake on a lower oven rack 25-30 minutes or until a knife inserted in the center comes out clean. Let stand 10 minutes before cutting.

1 SLICE: 394 cal., 26g fat (13g sat. fat), 209mg chol., 380mg sod., 21g carb. (3g sugars, 0 fiber), 17g pro.

NOTES

_____

_____

_____

_____

_____

_____

_____

_____

Elegant Smoked Salmon Strata

This overnight egg bake is ideal for guests. In the morning, simply let it come to room temperature and prepare a side dish as it bakes. Then get ready for compliments!
—*Lisa Speer, Palm Beach, FL*

PREP: 30 MIN. + CHILLING • **BAKE:** 55 MIN. + STANDING • **MAKES:** 12 SERVINGS

4 cups cubed ciabatta bread
2 Tbsp. butter, melted
2 Tbsp. olive oil
2 cups shredded Gruyere or Swiss cheese
2 cups shredded white cheddar cheese
10 green onions, sliced
½ lb. smoked salmon or lox, coarsely chopped
8 large eggs
4 cups 2% milk
4 tsp. Dijon mustard
¼ tsp. salt
¼ tsp. pepper
Creme fraiche or sour cream
Minced chives

1. In a large bowl, toss bread cubes with butter and oil; transfer to a greased 13x9-in. baking dish. Sprinkle with cheeses, onions and salmon. In another bowl, whisk the eggs, milk, mustard, salt and pepper; pour over top. Cover and refrigerate overnight.

2. Remove from the refrigerator 30 minutes before baking. Preheat oven to 350°. Cover and bake for 30 minutes. Uncover; bake until a knife inserted in the center comes out clean, 25-30 minutes longer. Let stand for 10 minutes before serving. Serve with creme fraiche and chives.

1 PIECE: 359 cal., 21g fat (11g sat. fat), 194mg chol., 845mg sod., 21g carb. (6g sugars, 1g fiber), 22g pro.

Cherry Fruit Smoothies

You need just four ingredients to blend together these super-fast smoothies. Try whipping them up on a hot summer day for a cool and refreshing treat.
—*Macy Plummer, Avon, IN*

TAKES: 5 MIN. • **MAKES:** 4 SERVINGS

1½ **cups unsweetened apple juice**
1 **cup frozen unsweetened raspberries**
1 **cup frozen pitted dark sweet cherries**
1½ **cups raspberry sherbet**

In a blender, combine the apple juice, raspberries and cherries. Add sherbet; cover and process until well blended. Pour into chilled glasses; serve immediately.

1 CUP: 160 cal., 2g fat (1g sat. fat), 3mg chol., 29mg sod., 37g carb. (31g sugars, 2g fiber), 2g pro.

Have a Heart

Show 'em some food love. These readers' sweet ideas tell your valentine everything you want to say.

"Begin their day with a fun-named favorite: toad in the hole. Use a cookie cutter to make a heart shape in the slice of bread."
—NANCY MURPHY, ONEONTA, NY

"After sleepovers, I often make heart-shaped pancakes for my kids and their friends."
—SANDY PEASE SMITH, BRIMSON, MO

Chocolate Lover's Pancakes

These indulgent chocolate pancakes are fluffy on the inside, with a rich but not-too-sweet flavor from the cocoa and a nice tang from the buttermilk. They're delicious with either maple or chocolate syrup—and even better with both swirled together on the plate!
—*Harland Johns, Leesburg, TX*

PREP: 15 MIN. • **COOK:** 5 MIN./BATCH • **MAKES:** 4 SERVINGS

1 cup all-purpose flour
¼ cup baking cocoa
2 Tbsp. sugar
1 tsp. baking powder
½ tsp. baking soda
½ tsp. salt
1 cup buttermilk
1 large egg, room temperature
2 Tbsp. butter, melted
1 tsp. vanilla extract
Maple syrup and chocolate syrup

1. In a large bowl, whisk flour, cocoa, sugar, baking powder, baking soda and salt. In another bowl, whisk buttermilk, egg, melted butter and vanilla until blended. Add to dry ingredients, stirring just until moistened.

2. Place a greased large nonstick skillet over medium heat. In batches, pour batter by ¼ cupfuls onto skillet; cook until bubbles on top begin to pop and bottoms are golden brown. Turn; cook until second side is golden brown. Serve with syrups.

2 PANCAKES: 271 cal., 8g fat (4g sat. fat), 64mg chol., 753mg sod., 42g carb. (16g sugars, 2g fiber), 8g pro.

Broccoli Quiche Cups

Make this crustless quiche in muffin cups or in a regular-size pie tin. Either way, there's plenty of bacony, cheesy goodness to go around.
—*Angela Lively, Conroe, TX*

TAKES: 25 MIN. • **MAKES:** 1 DOZEN

1 cup chopped fresh broccoli
1 cup shredded pepper jack cheese
6 large eggs, lightly beaten
¾ cup heavy whipping cream
½ cup bacon bits
1 shallot, minced
¼ tsp. salt
¼ tsp. pepper

1. Preheat oven to 350°. Divide broccoli and cheese among 12 greased muffin cups.

2. Whisk together remaining ingredients; pour into cups. Bake until set, 15-20 minutes.

2 QUICHE CUPS: 291 cal., 24g fat (12g sat. fat), 243mg chol., 523mg sod., 4g carb. (2g sugars, 0 fiber), 16g pro.

Strawberry-Hazelnut French Toast

My husband and I discovered this nutty French toast at a bed-and-breakfast in Arkansas. We bought their cookbook so we could make it at home. We've changed the recipe a bit over the years, but it still reminds us of that lovely inn.

—*Lynn Daniel, Dallas, TX*

PREP: 15 MIN. + CHILLING • BAKE: 35 MIN. • MAKES: 10 SERVINGS

½ cup butter, cubed
1 cup packed brown sugar
2 Tbsp. light corn syrup
10 slices French bread baguette (1 in. thick)
5 large eggs
1½ cups half-and-half cream
2 Tbsp. hazelnut liqueur or hazelnut syrup
1 Tbsp. vanilla extract
Sliced fresh strawberries and chopped hazelnuts

1. In a microwave, melt the butter with brown sugar and corn syrup; stir until brown sugar is blended. Pour into a greased 13x9-in. baking dish; top with bread.

2. In a large bowl, whisk eggs, cream, liqueur and vanilla; pour over bread. Refrigerate, covered, overnight.

3. Preheat oven to 350°. Remove French toast from refrigerator while oven heats. Bake, uncovered, until edges are golden and a knife inserted in the center comes out clean, 35-40 minutes. Let stand 5-10 minutes before serving. Serve with strawberries and hazelnuts.

1 SERVING: 304 cal., 15g fat (9g sat. fat), 135mg chol., 184mg sod., 34g carb. (29g sugars, 0 fiber), 5g pro.

Easy Glazed Bacon

Brown sugar, mustard and wine make bacon a little more special in this recipe. It's easy to prepare while working on the rest of the meal.

—*Judith Dobson, Burlington, WI*

PREP: 10 MIN. • BAKE: 30 MIN. • MAKES: 8 SERVINGS

1 lb. sliced bacon
1 cup packed brown sugar
¼ cup white wine or unsweetened apple juice
2 Tbsp. Dijon mustard

1. Preheat oven to 350°. Place bacon on a rack in an ungreased 15x10x1-in. baking pan. Bake 10 minutes; drain.

2. Combine brown sugar, wine and mustard; drizzle half over bacon. Bake 10 minutes. Turn bacon and drizzle with remaining glaze. Bake 10 minutes or until golden brown. Place bacon on waxed paper until set. Serve warm.

2 BACON STRIPS: 221 cal., 10g fat (3g sat. fat), 16mg chol., 404mg sod., 27g carb. (27g sugars, 0 fiber), 6g pro.

Banana Cream Eclairs

To surprise my banana-loving family, I made these for a reunion.
They're special treats that look and taste delicious.
—*Ruby Williams, Bogalusa, LA*

PREP: 40 MIN. • **BAKE:** 25 MIN. + COOLING • **MAKES:** 16 SERVINGS

1 cup water
½ cup butter, cubed
¼ cup sugar
½ tsp. salt
1 cup all-purpose flour
4 large eggs, room
temperature

FILLING
2½ cups heavy whipping
cream
3 Tbsp. sugar
1 tsp. vanilla extract
3 to 4 medium firm
bananas

GLAZE
½ cup confectioners'
sugar
2 Tbsp. baking cocoa
2 Tbsp. butter, melted
1 tsp. vanilla extract
1 to 2 Tbsp. boiling water
½ cup finely chopped
pecans

1. In a large saucepan, bring the water, butter, sugar and salt to a boil. Add flour all at once and stir until a smooth ball forms. Remove from the heat; let stand for 5 minutes. Add eggs, 1 at a time, beating well after each addition. Continue beating until dough is smooth and shiny.

2. Insert a ¾-in. round tip into a pastry bag; add dough. Pipe 3-in. strips about 3 in. apart on a greased baking sheet. Bake at 400° for 25-30 minutes or until golden brown. Remove to wire racks. Immediately split puffs open; remove tops and set aside. Discard soft dough from inside. Cool puffs.

3. In a large bowl, beat cream until it begins to thicken. Add sugar and vanilla; beat until stiff peaks form. In another bowl, mash bananas; gently fold in whipped cream. Spoon into eclairs; replace tops.

4. In a small bowl, combine the confectioners' sugar, cocoa, butter and vanilla. Add enough water to make a thin glaze. Spread over eclairs. Sprinkle with pecans. Refrigerate leftovers.

1 ECLAIR: 323 cal., 25g fat (14g sat. fat), 123mg chol., 176mg sod., 22g carb. (14g sugars, 1g fiber), 4g pro.

Sausage & Eggs over Cheddar-Parmesan Grits

These creamy grits topped with Italian sausage, peppers, onions and a fried egg are total comfort food. Perfect for brunch or a lazy dinner, they are easy to put together and will satisfy a hungry crew.
—*Debbie Glasscock, Conway, AR*

PREP: 20 MIN. • **COOK:** 20 MIN. • **MAKES:** 6 SERVINGS

1 lb. bulk Italian sausage
1 large sweet onion, chopped
1 medium sweet yellow pepper, chopped
1 medium sweet red pepper, chopped
6 cups water
1½ cups quick-cooking grits
1 cup shredded sharp cheddar cheese
½ cup shredded Parmesan cheese
2 Tbsp. half-and-half cream
½ tsp. salt
¼ tsp. pepper
2 tsp. olive oil
6 large eggs
Hot pepper sauce, optional

1. In a Dutch oven, cook sausage, onion, yellow pepper and red pepper over medium heat until sausage is no longer pink and vegetables are tender, 6-8 minutes, breaking up sausage into crumbles; drain.

2. Meanwhile, in a large saucepan, bring water to a boil. Slowly stir in grits. Reduce heat to medium-low; cook, covered, until thickened, about 5 minutes, stirring occasionally. Remove from heat. Stir in cheeses, cream, salt and pepper; keep warm.

3. In a large skillet, heat oil over medium-high heat. Break eggs, 1 at a time, into pan; reduce heat to low. Cook until whites are set and yolks begin to thicken, turning once if desired. Divide the grits among 6 serving bowls; top with sausage mixture and eggs. If desired, serve with pepper sauce.

1 SERVING: 538 cal., 32g fat (12g sat. fat), 253mg chol., 972mg sod., 38g carb. (5g sugars, 3g fiber), 26g pro.

Glazed Doughnut Holes

Here's a simple recipe to create a colorful and fun breakfast or snack. For the glaze, use any type of juice you like.
—Taste of Home *Test Kitchen*

PREP: 5 MIN. + STANDING • MAKES: 1 DOZEN

2 cups confectioners' sugar
3 to 5 Tbsp. frozen grape, cherry-pomegranate or cranberry juice concentrate, thawed
12 doughnut holes

LEMON VARIATION
2 cups confectioners' sugar
5 Tbsp. lemon juice

Whisk together sugar and enough juice concentrate to achieve a thick glaze. Dip doughnut holes in glaze; transfer to waxed paper.

1 DOUGHNUT HOLE: 225 cal., 4g fat (2g sat. fat), 1mg chol., 69mg sod., 49g carb. (44g sugars, 0 fiber), 1g pro.

LEMON DOUGHNUT HOLES For lemon glaze, whisk together sugar and lemon juice until smooth. Dip doughnut holes and transfer to waxed paper.

Brownie Batter Oatmeal

We've all grown up eating piping hot bowls of oatmeal for breakfast, and everyone has their favorite toppings to make porridge more palatable. My recipe transforms a ho-hum morning staple into something you'll jump out of bed for!
—*Kristen Moyer, Bethlehem, PA*

TAKES: 30 MIN. • MAKES: 2 SERVINGS

1 cup pitted dates, chopped
1 cup 2% milk
½ cup ground almonds
⅓ cup old-fashioned oats
2 Tbsp. baking cocoa
1 tsp. butter
1 tsp. vanilla extract
Optional: Fresh raspberries and sliced almonds

1. Place dates in a heatproof bowl; cover with boiling water. Let stand until softened, about 10 minutes. Drain, reserving ⅓ cup liquid. Place dates and reserved liquid in a food processor; process until smooth.

2. In a small saucepan, whisk milk, almonds, oats, cocoa and ¼ cup date puree until blended. (Save remaining puree for another use.) Bring to a boil over medium heat, stirring occasionally. Remove from heat; stir in butter and vanilla. If desired, garnish with raspberries and almonds.

¾ CUP: 338 cal., 18g fat (4g sat. fat), 15mg chol., 73mg sod., 37g carb. (19g sugars, 7g fiber), 12g pro.

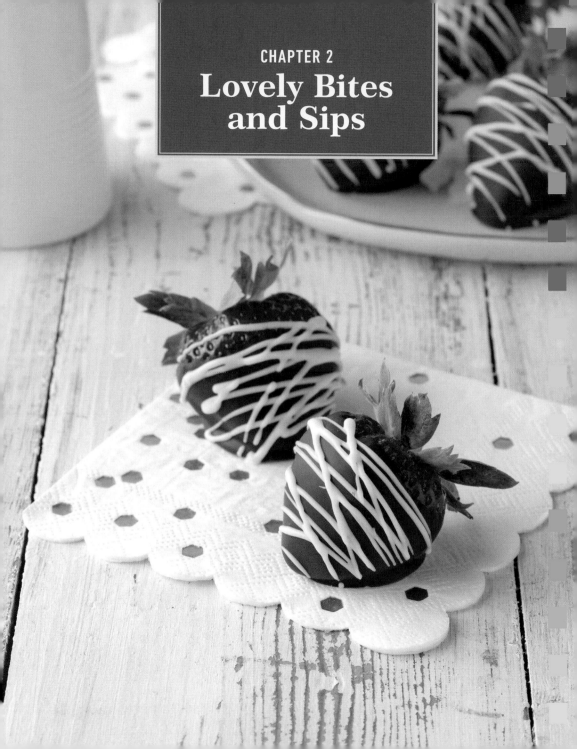

Chocolate-Dipped Strawberries

Plump berries from our strawberry patch turned into a real treat when I dipped them in chocolate! I like to make these before dinner and put them in the fridge, so they're ready to enjoy when we're finished eating.

—*Valerie Gee, Depew, NY*

TAKES: 20 MIN. • **MAKES:** ABOUT 9 STRAWBERRIES

1 **pint large strawberries**
4 **oz. semisweet chocolate, chopped**
1 **Tbsp. plus ½ tsp. shortening, divided**
1 **oz. white baking chocolate**
4 **drops food coloring, optional**

1. Wash strawberries and gently pat with paper towels until completely dry. In a microwave-safe bowl, melt semisweet chocolate and 1 Tbsp. shortening at 50% power; stir until smooth. Dip each strawberry and place on a waxed paper-lined baking sheet. Freeze strawberries for 5 minutes.

2. Meanwhile, microwave white chocolate and remaining shortening at 30% power until melted; stir until smooth. Stir in food coloring if desired. Drizzle over strawberries. Refrigerate until serving.

1 BERRY: 57 cal., 4g fat (2g sat. fat), 1mg chol., 4mg sod., 6g carb. (5g sugars, 1g fiber), 1g pro.

OUR FAVORITE PINK WINES TO POP ON VALENTINE'S DAY
It's time to think pink—pink wine, that is! These are our sommelier's top picks for gorgeous rosés to uncork with your special someone.

- Jansz Premium Rosé Brut NV
- Planeta Rosé
- Round Barn Cherry Spritzer
- Chandon Sparkling Rosé Brut NV
- Couly-Dutheil René Couly Chinon Rosé
- Beckmen Vineyards PMV Grenache Rosé
- Launois Brut Rosé Champagne NV
- Bellavista Sparkling Rosé
- Bird in Hand Rosé
- Caprock Rainy Rosé
- Clos Cibonne Rosé Tradition
- Brown Estate Duppy Conqueror Rosé
- Inniskillin Cabernet Franc Icewine

Bee My Honey Fruit Dip

Orange, cinnamon and nutmeg round out this creamy spiced dip.
I serve it with apples, pineapple and strawberries.
—*Carol Gillespie, Chambersburg, PA*

TAKES: 5 MIN. • **MAKES:** 2 CUPS

1 pkg. (8 oz.) cream
   cheese, softened
1 jar (7 oz.) marshmallow
   creme
1 Tbsp. honey
1 tsp. grated orange zest
¼ tsp. ground cinnamon
⅛ tsp. ground nutmeg
   Assorted fresh fruit

In a small bowl, beat the first 6 ingredients until smooth. Serve with fruit. Refrigerate leftovers.

2 TBSP.: 95 cal., 5g fat (3g sat. fat), 16mg chol., 52mg sod., 12g carb. (10g sugars, 0 fiber), 1g pro.

Rosemary Strawberry Daiquiri

This strawberry daiquiri is a standout with its herbal twist! I used to teach herb classes at our local technical college and everyone enjoyed my segment on herbal cocktails, including this one.
—*Sue Gronholz, Beaver Dam, WI*

PREP: 20 MIN. + COOLING • **MAKES:** 8 SERVINGS

1 cup sugar
1 cup water
4 fresh rosemary sprigs

EACH SERVING
1 cup frozen
   unsweetened sliced
   strawberries
1½ oz. white rum
1 oz. lime juice
   Whole fresh
   strawberries and
   rosemary sprigs

1. In a small saucepan, bring sugar and water to a boil. Reduce heat; simmer 10 minutes. Remove from heat; add rosemary. Steep, covered, 10-15 minutes according to taste. Discard rosemary. Cool completely. Store in an airtight container in the refrigerator up to 1 month.

2. For each serving, in a blender, combine the frozen strawberries, rum, lime juice and 2 Tbsp. rosemary syrup; cover and process until smooth. Pour into a chilled glass; garnish with a whole strawberry and an additional sprig of rosemary.

1 SERVING: 251 cal., 0 fat (0 sat. fat), 0 chol., 1mg sod., 41g carb. (32g sugars, 3g fiber), 0 pro.

Oysters Rockefeller

My husband and I are oyster farmers, and we delight our guests with this classic dish that originated in New Orleans. It's deliciously simple!
—*Beth Walton, Eastham, MA*

PREP: 1¼ HOURS • BAKE: 10 MIN. • MAKES: 3 DOZEN

1 medium onion, finely chopped
½ cup butter, cubed
1 pkg. (9 oz.) fresh spinach, torn
1 cup grated Romano cheese
1 Tbsp. lemon juice
⅛ tsp. pepper
2 lbs. kosher salt
3 dozen fresh oysters in the shell, washed

1. In a large skillet, saute onion in butter until tender. Add spinach; cook and stir until wilted. Remove from the heat; stir in cheese, lemon juice and pepper.

2. Spread kosher salt into 2 ungreased 15x10x1-in. baking pans. Shuck the oysters, reserving oyster and its liquid in bottom shell. Lightly press oyster shells down into the salt, using salt to keep oysters level. Top each with 2½ tsp. spinach mixture.

3. Bake, uncovered, at 450° until the oysters are plump, 6-8 minutes. Serve immediately.

1 OYSTER: 79 cal., 5g fat (3g sat. fat), 32mg chol., 133mg sod., 3g carb. (0 sugars, 0 fiber), 6g pro.

NOTES

_____

_____

_____

_____

_____

_____

_____

Bacon Water Chestnut Wraps

In our house, no celebration is complete without these classic bacon wraps.
It's impossible to eat just one!
—*Laura Mahaffey, Annapolis, MD*

PREP: 20 MIN. • BAKE: 30 MIN. • MAKES: ABOUT 2½ DOZEN

1 **lb. bacon strips**
2 **cans (8 oz. each) whole water chestnuts, drained**
½ **cup packed brown sugar**
½ **cup mayonnaise**
¼ **cup chili sauce**

1. Cut bacon strips in half. In a large skillet over medium heat, cook bacon until almost crisp; drain. Wrap each bacon piece around a water chestnut and secure with a toothpick. Place in an ungreased 13x9-in. baking dish.

2. In a small bowl, combine brown sugar, mayonnaise and chili sauce; pour over water chestnuts. Bake, uncovered, at 350° for 30 minutes or until hot and bubbly.

1 APPETIZER: 75 cal., 5g fat (1g sat. fat), 6mg chol., 148mg sod., 6g carb. (4g sugars, 0 fiber), 2g pro.

READER REVIEW
"I've taken this to several parties, and it is always the first to go! Love it!"
—CLCROW, TASTEOFHOME.COM

NOTES

_____
_____
_____
_____
_____
_____
_____
_____
_____
_____

Soft-Hearted Hello

Extend a warm and fluffy welcome, starting
with the front door.

WHAT YOU'LL NEED
Yarn (1-2 skeins of each of 3 colors)
Heart-shaped foam wreath form
Card stock
Pink acrylic paint
Pompom maker
Hot glue gun
Paintbrush

DIRECTIONS
1. Make approximately
70 pompoms using instructions with
pompom maker, keeping most 3½ cm in diameter,
some 5½ cm, and a few 7 cm.

2. Hot-glue pompoms to wreath form. Glue smallest pompoms
along inner edge to keep heart shape in the middle.

3. To make envelope detail, cut a 2x2¾-in. card stock rectangle.
Draw flaps with a marker. Draw a heart in center; paint with
2 coats of acrylic paint, drying thoroughly between coats.

4. Hot-glue envelope to wreath.

Champagne Cocktail

This festive drink is a champagne twist on the traditional old-fashioned.
Try it with extra dry champagne.
—Taste of Home *Test Kitchen*

TAKES: 5 MIN. • MAKES: 1 SERVING

1 **sugar cube or ½ tsp.
  sugar**
6 **dashes bitters**
½ **oz. brandy**
½ **cup chilled champagne
  Fresh rosemary sprig
  and fresh or frozen
  cranberries, optional**

Place sugar in a champagne flute or cocktail glass;
sprinkle with bitters. Add brandy; top with champagne.
If desired, top with rosemary and cranberries.

1 SERVING: 130 cal., 0 fat (0 sat. fat), 0 chol., 0 sod., 5g carb.
(2g sugars, 0 fiber), 0 pro.

Cucumber-Stuffed Cherry Tomatoes

Here's a wonderful appetizer that you can make ahead. It's the perfect use for homegrown
cherry tomatoes. I often triple the recipe because they disappear fast.
—*Christi Martin, Elko, NV*

TAKES: 25 MIN. • MAKES: 2 DOZEN

24 **cherry tomatoes**
3 **oz. cream cheese,
  softened**
2 **Tbsp. mayonnaise**
¼ **cup finely chopped
  peeled cucumber**
1 **Tbsp. finely chopped
  green onion**
2 **tsp. minced fresh dill**

1. Cut a thin slice off the top of each tomato. Scoop out and
discard pulp; invert tomatoes onto paper towels to drain.

2. In a small bowl, combine cream cheese and mayonnaise
until smooth; stir in the cucumber, onion and dill. Spoon
into tomatoes. Refrigerate until serving.

1 STUFFED TOMATO. 25 cal., 2g fat (1g sat. fat), 4mg chol.,
18mg sod., 1g carb. (1g sugars, 0 fiber), 0 pro. **DIABETIC
EXCHANGES:** ½ fat.

Chocolate Pecan Fondue

When our kids have friends sleep over, I surprise them with this chocolate treat. Our favorite dippers include fruit, marshmallows, cookies and pound cake.
—*Suzanne McKinley, Lyons, GA*

TAKES: 15 MIN. • **MAKES:** 1⅓ CUPS

½ cup half-and-half cream
2 Tbsp. honey
9 oz. semisweet chocolate, broken into small pieces
¼ cup finely chopped pecans
1 tsp. vanilla extract
Fresh fruit and shortbread cookies

1. In a heavy saucepan over low heat, combine cream and honey; heat until warm. Add chocolate; stir until melted. Stir in pecans and vanilla.

2. Transfer to a fondue pot or a 1½-qt. slow cooker and keep warm. Serve with fruit and cookies.

2 TBSP.: 178 cal., 12g fat (6g sat. fat), 6mg chol., 6mg sod., 19g carb. (17g sugars, 2g fiber), 3g pro.

Blue Cheese-Stuffed Shrimp

Jumbo shrimp becomes even more extraordinary when stuffed with blue cheese. The mild flavor has mass appeal.
—*Amy Dollimount, Glace Bay, NS*

PREP: 20 MIN. + CHILLING • **MAKES:** 2 DOZEN

3 oz. cream cheese, softened
⅔ cup minced fresh parsley, divided
¼ cup crumbled blue cheese
1 tsp. chopped shallot
½ tsp. Creole mustard
24 cooked jumbo shrimp, peeled and deveined

1. In a small bowl, beat cream cheese until smooth. Beat in ⅓ cup of the parsley, blue cheese, shallot and mustard. Refrigerate at least 1 hour.

2. Make a deep slit along the back of each shrimp to within ¼ to ½ in. of the bottom. Stuff with cream cheese mixture; press remaining parsley onto cream cheese mixture.

1 STUFFED SHRIMP: 43 cal., 2g fat (1g sat. fat), 54mg chol., 89mg sod., 0 carb. (0 sugars, 0 fiber), 6g pro. **DIABETIC EXCHANGES:** 1 meat.

Double Chocolate Martini

Is it a beverage or a dessert? Don't let its sweet looks fool you;
this chocolate martini is potent! And it's so good.
—*Deborah Williams, Peoria, AZ*

TAKES: 5 MIN. • **MAKES:** 1 SERVING

Grated chocolate
1 maraschino cherry
Chocolate syrup,
    optional
Ice cubes
2½ oz. half-and-half cream
1½ oz. vodka
1½ oz. chocolate liqueur
1½ oz. creme de cacao

1. Sprinkle grated chocolate on a plate. Moisten the rim of a martini glass with water; hold glass upside down and dip rim into the chocolate. Place cherry in glass. If desired, garnish glass with chocolate syrup.

2. Fill a tumbler or mixing glass three-fourths full with ice. Add the cream, vodka, chocolate liqueur and creme de cacao; stir until condensation forms on outside of tumbler. Strain into glass; serve immediately.

1 SERVING: 717 cal., 8g fat (5g sat. fat), 38mg chol., 49mg sod., 60g carb. (26g sugars, 0 fiber), 3g pro.

Caprese Salad Kabobs

Trade in the usual veggie party platter for these fun kabobs. I often make these
for my family to snack on, and it's a great recipe for the kids to help with.
—*Christine Mitchell, Glendora, CA*

TAKES: 10 MIN. • **MAKES:** 12 KABOBS

24 grape tomatoes
12 cherry-size fresh
    mozzarella cheese
    balls
24 fresh basil leaves
2 Tbsp. olive oil
2 tsp. balsamic vinegar

On each of 12 appetizer skewers, alternately thread 2 tomatoes, 1 cheese ball and 2 basil leaves. Whisk olive oil and vinegar; drizzle over kabobs.

1 KABOB: 44 cal., 4g fat (1g sat. fat), 5mg chol., 10mg sod., 2g carb. (1g sugars, 0 fiber), 1g pro. **DIABETIC EXCHANGES:** 1 fat.

Steak & Blue Cheese Bruschetta with Onion & Roasted Tomato Jam

Some of my favorite steakhouse flavors—ribeye, tomato, sweet onion and blue cheese—inspired this bruschetta. It's hearty, delicious and shows up at all our parties and special gatherings.
—*Debbie Reid, Clearwater, FL*

PREP: 45 MIN. • **GRILL:** 10 MIN. • **MAKES:** 16 APPETIZERS

5 Tbsp. olive oil, divided
1 large sweet onion, halved and thinly sliced
1 cup grape tomatoes, halved
½ tsp. kosher salt, divided
¼ tsp. freshly ground pepper, divided
6 oz. cream cheese, softened
¾ cup crumbled blue cheese
3 garlic cloves, minced
16 slices French bread baguette (½ in. thick)
2 beef ribeye steaks (¾ in. thick and 8 oz. each)
1½ tsp. Montreal steak seasoning
2 Tbsp. balsamic vinegar

1. Preheat oven to 400°. In large skillet, heat 2 Tbsp. oil over medium-high heat; saute onion until softened. Reduce heat to medium-low; cook until golden brown, 25-30 minutes, stirring occasionally.

2. Toss tomatoes with 1 Tbsp. oil, ¼ tsp. salt and ⅛ tsp. pepper; spread in a 15x10x1-in. pan. Roast until softened, 10-15 minutes. Stir tomatoes into onion, mashing lightly. In small bowl, mix cream cheese, blue cheese, garlic and the remaining salt and pepper.

3. Brush bread slices with remaining oil; grill, covered, over medium heat until lightly toasted, 1-2 minutes per side. Sprinkle steaks with steak seasoning. Grill, covered, over medium heat until meat reaches desired doneness (for medium-rare, a thermometer should read 135°; medium, 140°; medium-well, 145°), 3-5 minutes per side. Let stand 5 minutes before slicing.

4. To serve, spread toasts with cheese mixture; top with steak and onion mixture. Drizzle with vinegar.

1 APPETIZER: 185 cal., 14g fat (6g sat. fat), 32mg chol., 292mg sod., 7g carb. (2g sugars, 0 fiber), 8g pro.

Rhubarb Lemonade Slush

My family loves rhubarb, and this is such a fun way to enjoy it. It's nice to have in the freezer and bring out when guests drop by. Even people who aren't crazy about rhubarb enjoy it.
—*Cathie Beard, Philomath, OR*

PREP: 30 MIN. + FREEZING • **MAKES:** 12 SERVINGS

3 **cups chopped fresh or frozen rhubarb**
1 **cup water**
⅓ **cup sugar**
1 **cup vodka**
¾ **cup thawed pink lemonade concentrate**
1 **bottle (2 liters) lemon-lime soda, chilled**

1. In a large saucepan, bring rhubarb, water and sugar to a boil. Reduce heat, simmer, covered, 5 minutes or until rhubarb is tender. Cool slightly.

2. Puree mixture in a blender; transfer to a 1-qt. freezer container. Stir in vodka and lemonade concentrate. Freeze, covered, until firm, at least 8 hours.

3. To serve, transfer mixture to a pitcher; stir in soda. Or, for each serving, place ⅓ cup rhubarb mixture in an 8-oz. glass; stir in ⅔ cup soda.

1 CUP: 180 cal., 0 fat (0 sat. fat), 0 chol., 19mg sod., 35g carb. (31g sugars, 1g fiber), 0 pro.

NOTES

CHAPTER 3
A Match Made in Heaven

Turkey Sandwich with Raspberry-Mustard Spread

Get cozy with your special someone when you pair this delightful sandwich with a cup of soup. Filled with flavor, it's a delicious idea for a valentine surprise in lunch bags, too!

—Sarah Savage, Buena Vista, VA

TAKES: 25 MIN. • MAKES: 2 SERVINGS

1 Tbsp. honey
1 Tbsp. spicy brown mustard
1 tsp. red raspberry preserves
¼ tsp. mustard seed
1 Tbsp. olive oil
4 oz. fresh mushrooms, thinly sliced
1 cup fresh baby spinach, coarsely chopped
1 garlic clove, minced
½ tsp. chili powder
4 slices multigrain bread, toasted
6 oz. sliced cooked turkey breast
½ medium ripe avocado, sliced

1. Combine the honey, mustard, preserves and mustard seed; set aside. In a large skillet, heat oil over medium-high heat. Add mushrooms; cook and stir until tender, 4-5 minutes. Add spinach, garlic and chili powder; cook and stir until spinach is wilted, 3-4 minutes.

2. Spread half of the mustard mixture over 2 slices of toast. Layer with turkey, mushroom mixture and avocado. Spread remaining mustard mixture over remaining toast; place over top.

1 SANDWICH: 449 cal., 16g fat (3g sat. fat), 68mg chol., 392mg sod., 40g carb. (14g sugars, 7g fiber), 35g pro.

NOTES

Broccoli Cheddar Soup

Here's a fast, heartwarming delight that's simply perfect for two. Served with crusty bread and a green salad, it makes any night of the week feel extra special.
—*Cheryl McRae, West Valley, UT*

TAKES: 20 MIN. • **MAKES:** 2 SERVINGS

¼ cup chopped onion
¼ cup butter, cubed
¼ cup all-purpose flour
¼ tsp. salt
¼ tsp. pepper
1½ cups 2% milk
¾ cup chicken broth
1 cup cooked chopped
   fresh or frozen broccoli
½ cup shredded
   cheddar cheese

1. In a small saucepan, saute onion in butter until tender. Stir in the flour, salt and pepper until blended; gradually add milk and broth. Bring to a boil; cook and stir until thickened, about 2 minutes.

2. Add broccoli. Cook and stir until heated through. Remove from the heat; stir in cheese until melted.

1 CUP: 494 cal., 37g fat (24g sat. fat), 116mg chol., 1145mg sod., 26g carb. (11g sugars, 2g fiber), 16g pro.

READER REVIEW
"I made this for dinner and it was delicious! Of course I doubled the recipe because I love leftovers. Amazing soup! I will be sharing this with my friends and family."
—AMYJO65, TASTEOFHOME.COM

Grilled Caprese Quesadillas

These quick and easy quesadillas make great use of brilliant red tomatoes.
Feel free to swap in goat cheese or feta for the fresh mozzarella.
—*Amy Mongiovi, Lititz, PA*

TAKES: 20 MIN. • MAKES: 2 SERVINGS

4 whole wheat tortillas (8 in.)
6 oz. fresh mozzarella cheese, sliced
2 medium tomatoes, sliced and patted dry
⅓ cup julienned fresh basil
¼ cup pitted Greek olives, chopped
   Freshly ground pepper to taste

1. Layer half of each tortilla with cheese and tomatoes; sprinkle with basil, olives and pepper to taste. Fold tortillas to close.

2. Grill, covered, over medium-high heat until lightly browned and cheese is melted, 2-3 minutes per side.

1 QUESADILLA: 535 cal., 25g fat (13g sat. fat), 67mg chol., 665mg sod., 52g carb. (5g sugars, 8g fiber), 25g pro.

Champion Roast Beef Sandwiches

When I have time, I like to prepare a roast with this much-requested recipe in mind. But when I need a special meal in a hurry, I use deli roast beef with delicious results.
—*Ann Eastman, Santa Monica, CA*

TAKES: 15 MIN. • MAKES: 4 SERVINGS

½ cup sour cream
1 Tbsp. onion soup mix
1 Tbsp. prepared horseradish, drained
⅛ tsp. pepper
8 slices rye or pumpernickel bread
½ lb. sliced roast beef
Lettuce leaves

In a small bowl, combine the first 4 ingredients. Spread 1 Tbsp. on each slice of bread. Top 4 slices of bread with roast beef and lettuce; cover with remaining bread.

1 SANDWICH: 318 cal., 11g fat (6g sat. fat), 60mg chol., 1401mg sod., 34g carb. (4g sugars, 4g fiber), 18g pro.

Raspberry Pecan Chicken Salad

I gave this sweet-savory chicken salad a little zip with Chinese five-spice powder, which tastes a bit like pumpkin pie spice. Scoop this sandwich filling onto buttery croissants and serve with fresh fruit or a cup of soup.
—*Lisa Renshaw, Kansas City, MO*

TAKES: 15 MIN. • MAKES: 6 SANDWICHES

1 carton (6 oz.) orange yogurt
½ cup mayonnaise
¼ tsp. Chinese five-spice powder
3 cups cubed cooked chicken
2 green onions, chopped
¼ cup sliced celery
¼ cup chopped pecans, toasted
1 cup fresh raspberries
12 slices multigrain bread

In a large bowl, mix yogurt, mayonnaise and five-spice powder. Stir in chicken, green onions, celery and pecans. Gently stir in raspberries. Serve on bread.

1 SERVING: 463 cal., 24g fat (4g sat. fat), 65mg chol., 371mg sod., 31g carb. (10g sugars, 6g fiber), 29g pro.

Asparagus Soup with Lemon Creme Fraiche

Here is a definite winner—a silky-smooth fresh asparagus soup. Serve it warm or chilled depending on your preference.

—*Fern Vitense, Tipton, IA*

PREP: 25 MIN. • **COOK:** 25 MIN. • **MAKES:** 6 SERVINGS

1 Tbsp. butter
1 Tbsp. olive oil
1 small onion, chopped
4 cups cut fresh asparagus (1-in. pieces)
3 medium red potatoes, peeled and cubed
2 cans (14½ oz. each) vegetable broth
2 tsp. grated lemon zest
½ tsp. salt
½ tsp. pepper
½ tsp. ground coriander
¼ tsp. ground ginger

GARNISH
¼ cup minced chives
¼ cup creme fraiche or sour cream
1 Tbsp. lemon juice
½ tsp. grated lemon zest

1. In a large saucepan, heat the butter and olive oil over medium-high heat. Add onion; cook and stir until tender. Add asparagus and potatoes; cook 3 minutes longer. Stir in vegetable broth, lemon zest and seasonings. Bring to a boil. Reduce the heat; simmer, covered, until potatoes are tender, 15-20 minutes.

2. Cool slightly. Process soup in batches in a blender until smooth. Return all to the pan and heat through. Combine garnish ingredients; serve with soup.

1 CUP: 155 cal., 8g fat (4g sat. fat), 13mg chol., 873mg sod., 17g carb. (4g sugars, 3g fiber), 4g pro.

Peanut Butter, Strawberry & Honey Sandwich

Who needs jam when you have fresh strawberries? A drizzle of honey and a bit of mint make this sandwich stand out. What a great way to show someone how much you care!

—James Schend, Pleasant Prairie, WI

TAKES: 5 MIN. • MAKES: 1 SERVING

1 Tbsp. creamy peanut butter
1 slice crusty white bread
¼ cup sliced fresh strawberries
1 tsp. thinly sliced fresh mint
1 tsp. honey

Spread peanut butter over bread. Top with strawberries and mint; drizzle with honey.

1 OPEN-FACED SANDWICH: 208 cal., 9g fat (2g sat. fat), 0 chol., 211mg sod., 27g carb. (11g sugars, 2g fiber), 6g pro.

Chilled Raspberry Soup

Family and friends always enjoy sipping this pretty pink soup. I often use sugar substitute and reduced-fat sour cream to make it a little lighter.

—Amy Wenger, Severance, CO

PREP: 20 MIN. + CHILLING • MAKES: 12 SERVINGS

⅓ cup cranberry juice
⅓ cup sugar
5⅓ cups plus 12 fresh raspberries, divided
1⅓ cups plus 2 Tbsp. sour cream, divided

1. In a blender, combine the cranberry juice, sugar and 5⅓ cups raspberries; cover and process until blended. Strain and discard seeds. Stir in 1⅓ cups sour cream. Cover and refrigerate for at least 2 hours.

2. To serve, pour ¼ cup of soup into 12 cordial glasses. Top each with a raspberry and ½ tsp. sour cream.

¼ CUP: 111 cal., 5g fat (3g sat. fat), 19mg chol., 10mg sod., 14g carb. (10g sugars, 4g fiber), 2g pro.

Quick Tomato Soup

My family often requests my sweet homemade tomato soup on cold winter days.
It's great with a sandwich and nearly as quick to fix as the canned variety.
—*Jane Ward, Churchville, MD*

TAKES: 15 MIN. • MAKES: 6 SERVINGS

¼ cup butter
¼ cup all-purpose flour
1 tsp. curry powder
¼ tsp. onion powder
1 can (46 oz.) tomato juice
¼ cup sugar
Oyster crackers or croutons, optional

In a large saucepan, melt butter. Stir in flour, curry powder and onion powder until smooth. Gradually add tomato juice and sugar. Cook, uncovered, until thickened and heated through, about 5 minutes. If desired, serve with crackers or croutons.

1 CUP: 156 cal., 8g fat (5g sat. fat), 20mg chol., 862mg sod., 22g carb. (15g sugars, 1g fiber), 2g pro.

Sweet Bookmarks

Use a heart-shaped punch or scissors to cut hearts from patterned paper. Similarly, punch or cut smaller hearts from plain paper. Pen a message to your sweetie on the smaller hearts. Use adhesive to glue hearts together.

French Onion Soup with Swiss-Topped Toast

The key to a delicious French onion soup is a dark, savory broth. It's usually made with beef broth, but I think my vegetarian version is a winner.
—*Paul DeBenedictis, Reading, MA*

PREP: 30 MIN. • COOK: 1 HOUR 20 MINUTES • MAKES: 6 SERVINGS

- 3 lbs. yellow onions
- 1 lb. sweet onions, thinly sliced
- 2 Tbsp. butter
- 1 Tbsp. olive oil
- 1 tsp. dried thyme
- 1 tsp. brown sugar
- 1 tsp. balsamic vinegar
- 1 Tbsp. all-purpose flour
- 1 can (14½ oz.) vegetable broth
- 1 can (12 oz.) beer or 12 oz. vegetable broth
- ¼ cup white wine or additional vegetable broth
- 2 Tbsp. reduced-sodium soy sauce
- 1 Tbsp. Worcestershire sauce
- 2 tsp. brandy
- ½ tsp. coarsely ground pepper
- ¼ tsp. salt
- ⅛ tsp. cayenne pepper
- 6 slices French bread (1 in. thick)
- 6 slices Swiss cheese

1. In a Dutch oven, saute onions in butter and oil until tender. Reduce heat to medium-low; cook for 1 hour or until golden brown, stirring occasionally. Stir in the thyme, brown sugar and vinegar.

2. Combine the flour and broth until blended. Gradually stir into the onion mixture. Stir in the beer, wine, soy sauce, Worcestershire sauce, brandy, pepper, salt and cayenne. Bring to a boil. Reduce heat; cover and simmer for 10 minutes.

3. Meanwhile, place bread on a baking sheet. Broil 4 in. from the heat for 2 minutes on each side or until toasted. Top each with a cheese slice; broil for 2-3 minutes or until cheese is melted and lightly browned. Ladle soup into bowls; garnish with cheese-topped toast.

1 CUP WITH 1 BREAD SLICE WITH CHEESE: 377 cal., 14g fat (8g sat. fat), 35mg chol., 875mg sod., 45g carb. (21g sugars, 6g fiber), 12g pro.

Heart-Topped Chicken Potpie Soup

My grandmother hand-wrote a cookbook, which included her amazing homemade pie crust. I added the delicious soup to come up with this recipe. The pastry hearts are so cute and make it perfect for Valentine's Day.
—*Karen LeMay, Seabrook, TX*

PREP: 20 MIN. + CHILLING • COOK: 20 MIN. • MAKES: 6 SERVINGS

2 cups all-purpose flour
1¼ tsp. salt
⅔ cup shortening
5 to 6 Tbsp. 2% milk

SOUP
2 Tbsp. butter
1 cup cubed peeled potatoes
1 cup chopped sweet onion
2 celery ribs, chopped
2 medium carrots, chopped
½ cup all-purpose flour
½ tsp. salt
¼ tsp. pepper
3 cans (14½ oz. each) chicken broth
2 cups shredded cooked chicken
1 cup frozen petite peas
1 cup frozen corn

1. In a large bowl, mix flour and salt; cut in shortening until crumbly. Gradually add milk, tossing with a fork until dough holds together when pressed. Shape into a disk; wrap in plastic. Refrigerate for 30 minutes or overnight.

2. On a lightly floured surface, roll the dough to ⅛-in. thickness. Using a floured 2½-in. heart-shaped or round cutter, cut 18 shapes. Place 1 in. apart on ungreased baking sheets. Bake at 425° for 8-11 minutes or until golden brown. Cool on a wire rack.

3. For soup, heat butter in a Dutch oven over medium-high heat. Add the potatoes, onion, celery and carrots; cook and stir for 5-7 minutes or until onion is tender.

4. Stir in the flour, salt and pepper until blended; gradually whisk in the broth. Bring to a boil over medium-high heat, stirring occasionally. Reduce heat; simmer, uncovered, for 8-10 minutes or until potatoes are tender. Stir in remaining ingredients; heat through. Serve with pastries.

1½ CUPS SOUP WITH 3 PASTRIES: 614 cal., 30g fat (9g sat. fat), 57mg chol., 1706mg sod., 60g carb. (7g sugars, 5g fiber), 23g pro.

Toasted Clubs with Dill Mayo

Simple to prepare, appealing to look at and loaded with flavor, this bistro-style sandwich couldn't be better! It's a casual but nice lunch.
—*Jenny Flake, Newport Beach, CA*

TAKES: 20 MIN. • MAKES: 2 SERVINGS

2 Tbsp. fat-free mayonnaise
¼ tsp. dill weed
¾ tsp. lemon juice, divided
⅛ tsp. pepper
4 slices whole wheat bread, toasted
4 thin slices deli roast beef
4 thin slices deli ham
2 slices reduced-fat provolone cheese
2 Bibb lettuce leaves
2 slices tomato
2 center-cut bacon strips, cooked and crumbled
¼ cup alfalfa sprouts
¼ medium ripe avocado, peeled and sliced

1. In a small bowl, combine the mayonnaise, dill, ¼ tsp. lemon juice and pepper; spread over toast. Layer 2 slices with roast beef, ham, cheese, lettuce, tomato, bacon and alfalfa sprouts.

2. Drizzle avocado with remaining lemon juice; place over sprouts. Top with remaining toast.

1 SANDWICH: 328 cal., 13g fat (4g sat. fat), 47mg chol., 1056mg sod., 29g carb. (6g sugars, 6g fiber), 26g pro.

READER REVIEW
"I made this a couple of weeks ago, and my hubby and I just loved it. It's a very hearty sandwich. I have made this three more times since then. That's how delish it is. If you haven't tried it yet, you are missing out on a very awesome sandwich."
—BABYBOOP, TASTEOFHOME.COM

CHAPTER 4
Stuck-on-You
Sides

Berry-Beet Salad

Here's a delightfully different salad that balances the earthy flavor of beets with the natural sweetness of berries. If you prefer, substitute crumbled feta for the goat cheese.
—*Amy Lyons, Mounds View, MN*

PREP: 20 MIN. • **BAKE:** 30 MIN. + COOLING • **MAKES:** 4 SERVINGS

1   **each fresh red and golden beets**
¼   **cup balsamic vinegar**
2   **Tbsp. walnut oil**
1   **tsp. honey**
    Dash salt
    Dash pepper
½   **cup sliced fresh strawberries**
½   **cup fresh raspberries**
½   **cup fresh blackberries**
3   **Tbsp. chopped walnuts, toasted**
1   **shallot, thinly sliced**
4   **cups torn mixed salad greens**
1   **oz. fresh goat cheese, crumbled**
1   **Tbsp. fresh basil, thinly sliced**

1. Place beets in an 8-in. square baking dish; add 1 in. of water. Cover and bake at 400° for 30-40 minutes or until tender.

2. Meanwhile, in a small bowl, whisk the vinegar, oil, honey, salt and pepper; set aside. Cool beets; peel and cut into thin slices.

3. In a large bowl, combine the beets, berries, walnuts and shallot. Pour dressing over beet mixture and toss gently to coat. Divide salad greens among 4 serving plates. Top with beet mixture; sprinkle with cheese and basil.

1 SERVING: 183 cal., 12g fat (2g sat. fat), 5mg chol., 124mg sod., 18g carb. (11g sugars, 5g fiber), 4g pro.

NOTES

_____

_____

_____

_____

_____

_____

Seasoned Oven Fries

For a speedy, health-conscious bite, treat your valentine to these fun wedges.
They're just as tasty as the deep-fried version, but with less mess.
—*Pat Fredericks, Oak Creek, WI*

TAKES: 25 MIN. • **MAKES:** 2 SERVINGS

2   **medium baking
    potatoes**
2   **tsp. butter, melted**
2   **tsp. canola oil**
¼   **tsp. seasoned salt
    Minced fresh parsley,
    optional**

1. Cut each potato lengthwise in half; cut each piece into 4 wedges. In a large shallow dish, combine the butter, oil and seasoned salt. Add potatoes; turn to coat.

2. Place potatoes in a single layer on a baking sheet coated with cooking spray. Bake at 450° until tender, turning once, 20-25 minutes. If desired, sprinkle with parsley.

8 WEDGES: 263 cal., 9g fat (3g sat. fat), 10mg chol., 242mg sod., 44g carb. (3g sugars, 4g fiber), 4g pro.

READER REVIEW
"This recipe is so simple, yet really good. The potatoes bake up really nice, and my family could not stop talking about how good they were. Destined to be a family favorite!"
—SHECOOKSALOT, TASTEOFHOME.COM

Molded Strawberry Salad

This refreshing salad has two layers—a pretty pink bottom that includes sour cream, and a ruby red top with strawberries and pineapple, making it ideal for Valentine's Day.
—*Gloria Grant, Sterling, IL*

PREP: 10 MIN. + CHILLING • **MAKES:** 8 SERVINGS

1 **pkg. (6 oz.) strawberry gelatin**
1½ **cups boiling water**
1 **pkg. (10 oz.) frozen sweetened sliced strawberries, thawed**
1 **can (8 oz.) unsweetened crushed pineapple**
1 **cup sour cream**
Optional: Leaf lettuce and fresh strawberries

1. In a large bowl, dissolve the gelatin in water. Add the strawberries and pineapple. Strain, reserving liquid and fruit. Set aside 1 cup of the liquid at room temperature.

2. Pour fruit and remaining liquid into a 5-cup ring mold or 9-in. square pan that has been coated with cooking spray. Cover and refrigerate until set, about 1 hour.

3. Whisk sour cream and reserved liquid; pour over top of gelatin. Cover and refrigerate until set.

4. Slice and place on individual plates, or unmold onto a serving platter. Garnish with lettuce and strawberries if desired.

1 PIECE: 182 cal., 5g fat (4g sat. fat), 20mg chol., 64mg sod., 31g carb. (30g sugars, 1g fiber), 3g pro.

Parmesan Creamed Spinach

This rich and creamy dish takes just minutes to make. If I'm expecting guests for a special meal, I'll simply double or triple the recipe.
—Leann Ross, San Tan Valley, AZ

TAKES: 20 MIN. • MAKES: 4 SERVINGS

½ lb. sliced fresh mushrooms
1 small onion, chopped
2 tsp. butter
2 tsp. olive oil
1 garlic clove, minced
¼ tsp. salt
¼ tsp. pepper
1 pkg. (9 oz.) fresh spinach
4 oz. cream cheese, cubed and softened
½ cup shredded Parmesan cheese

1. In a large cast-iron or other heavy skillet, saute the mushrooms and onion in butter and oil until tender. Add the garlic, salt and pepper; cook 1 minute longer.

2. Add spinach and cream cheese; cook and stir until cream cheese is smooth and spinach is wilted. Sprinkle with cheese.

½ CUP: 217 cal., 17g fat (10g sat. fat), 44mg chol., 470mg sod., 8g carb. (2g sugars, 2g fiber), 10g pro.

Crunchy Apple Side Salad

With apples, dried cranberries, crunchy walnuts and a light dressing, this is a great side for celebrations. Top leftovers with granola for a lovely bite in the morning.
—Kathy Armstrong, Post Falls, ID

TAKES: 15 MIN. • MAKES: 5 SERVINGS

⅓ cup fat-free sugar-free vanilla yogurt
⅓ cup reduced-fat whipped topping
¼ tsp. plus ⅛ tsp. ground cinnamon, divided
2 medium red apples, chopped
1 large Granny Smith apple, chopped
¼ cup dried cranberries
2 Tbsp. chopped walnuts

In a large bowl, combine the yogurt, whipped topping and ¼ tsp. cinnamon. Add apples and cranberries; toss to coat. Refrigerate until serving. Sprinkle with walnuts and remaining cinnamon before serving.

¾ CUP: 109 cal., 3g fat (1g sat. fat), 0 chol., 12mg sod., 22g carb. (16g sugars, 3g fiber), 2g pro. **DIABETIC EXCHANGES:** 1 fruit, ½ starch, ½ fat.

Creamy Bow Tie Pasta

Add a little zip to any intimate meal with this quick and saucy pasta dish. It's an excellent accompaniment with almost any meat or seafood.
—*Kathy Kittell, Lenexa, KS*

TAKES: 25 MIN. • MAKES: 2 SERVINGS

1 cup uncooked
   bow tie pasta
1½ tsp. butter
2¼ tsp. olive oil
1½ tsp. all-purpose flour
½ tsp. minced garlic
   Dash salt
   Dash dried basil
   Dash crushed red
   pepper flakes
3 Tbsp. 2% milk
2 Tbsp. chicken broth
1 Tbsp. water
2 Tbsp. shredded
   Parmesan cheese
1 Tbsp. sour cream

1. Cook pasta according to package directions. Meanwhile, in a small saucepan, melt butter. Stir in the oil, flour, garlic and seasonings until blended. Gradually add the milk, broth and water. Bring to a boil; cook and stir until slightly thickened, about 2 minutes.

2. Remove from the heat; stir in cheese and sour cream. Drain pasta; toss with sauce.

¾ CUP: 196 cal., 12g fat (5g sat. fat), 19mg chol., 252mg sod., 17g carb. (2g sugars, 1g fiber), 6g pro.

READER REVIEW
"So good. I added chicken and broccoli and made it a main dish. It was easy with ingredients that I normally have on hand."
—KIM0827, TASTEOFHOME.COM

Roasted Brussels Sprouts & Cauliflower

Hosting a large dinner this Valentine's Day? Try this side. My grandkids aren't huge fans of cauliflower but they can't get enough of this! They like it even more with golden cauliflower.
—*Patricia Hudson, Riverview, FL*

PREP: 25 MIN. • **COOK:** 20 MIN. • **MAKES:** 12 SERVINGS

8 bacon strips, chopped
6 garlic cloves, minced
1 Tbsp. olive oil
1 Tbsp. butter, melted
¼ tsp. kosher salt
¼ tsp. coarsely
   ground pepper
4 cups Brussels
   sprouts, halved
4 cups fresh
   cauliflowerets
¼ cup grated
   Parmesan cheese
   Additional grated
   Parmesan cheese,
   optional

1. In a large skillet, cook bacon over medium heat until crisp, stirring occasionally. Remove with a slotted spoon; drain on paper towels. Discard the drippings, reserving 1 Tbsp.

2. In a large bowl, mix the garlic, oil, butter, salt, pepper and reserved drippings. Add the Brussels sprouts and cauliflower; toss to coat. Transfer to 2 greased 15x10x1-in. baking pans.

3. Bake at 400° for 20-25 minutes. Sprinkle each pan with 2 Tbsp. cheese. Bake 5 minutes longer or until vegetables are tender. Sprinkle with bacon and, if desired, additional cheese.

½ CUP: 137 cal., 11g fat (4g sat. fat), 17mg chol., 221mg sod., 5g carb. (2g sugars, 2g fiber), 5g pro.

Twice-Baked Red Potatoes

Before my baby was born, I was in nesting mode and made lots of freezable recipes like these creamy red potatoes. The yogurt is a healthy swap for sour cream.
—*Valerie Cox, Secretary, MD*

PREP: 30 MIN. • **BAKE:** 25 MIN. • **MAKES:** 1 DOZEN

6 **large red potatoes (about 10 oz. each)**
½ **cup 1% milk**
½ **cup fat-free plain yogurt**
3 **Tbsp. butter, softened**
1½ **tsp. dried parsley flakes**
1½ **tsp. garlic-herb seasoning blend**
1 **tsp. salt**
¼ **tsp. coarsely ground pepper**
1 **cup shredded Monterey Jack cheese**

1. Preheat oven to 350°. Scrub potatoes; pierce each several times with a fork. Microwave, uncovered, on high until just tender, 10-12 minutes, turning once.

2. When potatoes are cool enough to handle, cut each lengthwise in half. Scoop out pulp, leaving ¼-in.-thick shells. Mash pulp with all ingredients except cheese.

3. Spoon into potato shells. Top with cheese. Bake until heated through, 25-30 minutes. If desired, broil 2-3 minutes until cheese is light golden brown.

½ **STUFFED POTATO:** 211 cal., 6g fat (4g sat. fat), 17mg chol., 322mg sod., 34g carb. (3g sugars, 4g fiber), 7g pro. **DIABETIC EXCHANGES:** 2 starch, 1 fat.

READER REVIEW
"Flavor bomb after flavor bomb! A keeper recipe all around. Made half the recipe because it's just the two of us. Should have made the whole thing! Ms. Valerie Cox, you hit it out of the park."
—ASNUNEZ, TASTEOFHOME.COM

Fluffy Cranberry Delight

This was originally my daughter's recipe, and she or I will make it for special get-togethers.
It's particularly pretty in a cut-glass bowl on a buffet.
—*Ruth Bolduc, Conway, NH*

PREP: 20 MIN. + CHILLING • MAKES: 10 SERVINGS

4 cups cranberries
1½ cups sugar
¾ cup water
1 envelope unflavored gelatin
¼ cup lemon juice
2 Tbsp. orange juice
1½ cups heavy whipping cream
3 Tbsp. confectioners' sugar
1 tsp. vanilla extract

1. In a saucepan, bring the cranberries, sugar and water to a boil. Reduce heat and cook until berries burst. Strain through a food mill or sieve into a large bowl.

2. Stir in the gelatin, lemon juice and orange juice. Cool until mixture coats the back of a spoon.

3. In a small bowl, whip cream until soft peaks form. Add confectioners' sugar and vanilla; beat until stiff peaks form. Fold into cranberry mixture. Chill until set.

1 SERVING: 273 cal., 13g fat (8g sat. fat), 49mg chol., 16mg sod., 39g carb. (36g sugars, 2g fiber), 2g pro.

Mushroom & Spinach Saute

Mushrooms and spinach make a super fast combination that's perfect for two.
It's easy to double or triple for larger gatherings.
—*Pauline Howard, Lago Vista, TX*

TAKES: 10 MIN. • MAKES: 2 SERVINGS

2 tsp. olive oil
2 cups sliced fresh mushrooms
2 garlic cloves, minced
1 pkg. (5 to 6 oz.) fresh baby spinach
⅛ tsp. salt
⅛ tsp. pepper

In a large skillet, heat oil over medium-high heat. Add the mushrooms; saute until tender, about 2 minutes. Add garlic; cook 1 minute longer. Add spinach in batches; cook and stir until wilted, about 1 minute. Season with salt and pepper. Serve immediately.

¾ CUP: 76 cal., 5g fat (1g sat. fat), 0mg chol., 208mg sod., 6g carb. (2g sugars, 2g fiber), 4g pro. **DIABETIC EXCHANGES:** 1 vegetable, 1 fat.

Red Cabbage with Bacon

If you've braised, marinated or served red cabbage raw, try it steamed, then toss with bacon and a tangy sauce. We serve this pretty side dish with pork or chicken.
—*Sherri Melotik, Oak Creek, WI*

TAKES: 25 MIN. • **MAKES:** 6 SERVINGS

1 medium head red cabbage (about 2 lbs.), shredded
8 bacon strips, chopped
1 small onion, quartered and thinly sliced
2 Tbsp. all-purpose flour
¼ cup packed brown sugar
½ cup water
¼ cup cider vinegar
1 tsp. salt
⅛ tsp. pepper

1. In a large saucepan, place steamer basket over 1 in. of water. Place cabbage in basket. Bring water to a boil. Reduce heat to maintain a simmer; steam, covered, just until tender, 6-8 minutes.

2. Meanwhile, in a large skillet, cook bacon over medium heat until crisp, stirring occasionally. Remove with a slotted spoon; drain on paper towels. Discard drippings, reserving 2 Tbsp. in pan.

3. Add onion to drippings; cook and stir over medium-high heat until tender, 4-6 minutes. Stir in the flour and brown sugar until blended. Gradually stir in water and the cider vinegar. Bring to a boil, stirring constantly; cook and stir until thickened, 1-2 minutes. Stir in cabbage, bacon, salt and pepper.

¾ CUP: 188 cal., 9g fat (3g sat. fat), 15mg chol., 635mg sod., 23g carb. (15g sugars, 3g fiber), 6g pro.

Heart-Shaped Cinnamon Coffee Cakes

You'll love to make this pretty coffee cake for Valentine's Day and anniversaries.
—Norma Hammond, Leland, IA

PREP: 40 MIN. + RISING • **BAKE:** 15 MIN. • **MAKES:** 2 COFFEE CAKES (8 SERVINGS EACH)

1 pkg. (¼ oz.) active dry yeast
¼ cup warm water (110° to 115°)
1 cup warm 2% milk (110° to 115°)
½ cup butter, melted
2 large eggs, room temperature, lightly beaten
¼ cup sugar
1 tsp. salt
3½ to 4 cups all-purpose flour

FILLING
¼ cup butter, melted
½ cup sugar
½ cup finely chopped walnuts
2 tsp. ground cinnamon

ICING
2 Tbsp. butter, softened
2 cups confectioners' sugar
1 tsp. vanilla extract
5 to 6 Tbsp. 2% milk

1. In a small bowl, dissolve yeast in warm water. In a large bowl, combine milk, ½ cup butter, eggs, sugar, salt and 2 cups of flour; beat on medium speed until smooth. Stir in enough remaining flour to form a soft dough. Turn onto a floured surface; knead until smooth and elastic, 6-8 minutes. Place in a greased bowl; turn once to grease top. Cover and rise in a warm place until doubled, about 1 hour.

2. Punch dough down; let rest for 10 minutes. Divide in half. On a floured surface, roll each portion into a 15x10-in. rectangle. Brush with butter. Combine remaining filling ingredients; sprinkle over each rectangle to within ½ in. of edges.

3. Roll up jelly-roll style, starting with a long side; pinch seams to seal. Place, seam side up, on 2 greased baking sheets. Fold each roll in half lengthwise with seams together, creating a stacked loaf.

4. Starting from the folded end, with scissors, make a lengthwise cut down the middle to within 1 in. of open ends. Open and lay flat arranging into a heart shape. Pinch ends at tip of heart to seal. Cover and let rise until doubled, about 30 minutes.

5. Bake at 350° until golden brown, 15-20 minutes. Cool on wire racks.

6. For icing, in a small bowl, beat butter, sugar and vanilla extract until smooth. Add enough milk to achieve desired consistency. Drizzle over hearts.

1 PIECE: 329 cal., 14g fat (7g sat. fat), 52mg chol., 247mg sod., 47g carb. (25g sugars, 1g fiber), 5g pro.

Buttermilk Angel Biscuits

When I make these slightly sweet biscuits, sometimes I cut them and fold over one side about a third of the way for a more traditional look.

—*Carol Holladay, Danville, AL*

PREP: 30 MIN. + STANDING • **BAKE:** 10 MIN. • **MAKES:** 2 DOZEN

2 pkg. (¼ oz. each) active dry yeast
¼ cup warm water (110° to 115°)
5¼ to 5½ cups self-rising flour
⅓ cup sugar
1 tsp. baking soda
1 cup shortening
1¾ cups buttermilk

1. In a small bowl, dissolve yeast in warm water. In a large bowl, whisk 5¼ cups flour, sugar and baking soda. Cut in shortening until mixture resembles coarse crumbs. Stir in buttermilk and yeast mixture to form a soft dough (dough will be sticky).

2. Turn onto a floured surface; knead gently 8-10 times, adding flour if needed. Roll dough to ¾-in. thickness; cut with a floured 2½-in. biscuit cutter. Place 2 in. apart on greased baking sheets. Let stand at room temperature 20 minutes.

3. Preheat oven to 450°. Bake 8-12 minutes or until golden brown. Serve warm.

1 BISCUIT: 180 cal., 8g fat (2g sat. fat), 1mg chol., 386mg sod., 23g carb. (4g sugars, 1g fiber), 3g pro.

Red Velvet Cinnamon Rolls

Turn a box of red velvet cake mix into this easy valentine treat. Adding yeast to the mix is a clever trick. The red rolls with bright white icing are especially welcome at brunches.
—*Erin Wright, Wallace, KS*

PREP: 20 MIN. + RISING • **BAKE:** 15 MIN. • **MAKES:** 12 SERVINGS

1 **pkg. red velvet cake mix (regular size)**
2½ to 3 **cups all-purpose flour**
1 **pkg. (¼ oz.) active dry yeast**
1¼ **cups warm water (120° to 130°)**
½ **cup packed brown sugar**
1 **tsp. ground cinnamon**
¼ **cup butter, melted**

ICING
2 **cups confectioners' sugar**
2 **Tbsp. butter, softened**
1 **tsp. vanilla extract**
3 to 5 **Tbsp. 2% milk**

1. Combine cake mix, 1 cup flour and yeast. Add water; beat on medium speed 2 minutes. Stir in enough of the remaining flour to form a soft dough (dough will be sticky). Turn onto a lightly floured surface; knead gently 6-8 times. Place in a greased bowl, turning once to grease the top. Cover and let rise in a warm place until doubled, about 2 hours. Meanwhile, in another bowl, mix brown sugar and cinnamon.

2. Punch down dough. Turn onto a lightly floured surface; roll dough into an 18x10-in. rectangle. Brush with melted butter to within ¼ in. of edges; sprinkle with sugar mixture.

3. Roll up jelly-roll style, starting with a long side; pinch seam to seal. Cut crosswise into 12 slices. Place cut sides up in a greased 13x9-in. baking pan. Cover with a kitchen towel; let rise in a warm place until almost doubled, about 1 hour.

4. Preheat oven to 350°. Bake until puffed and light brown, 15-20 minutes. Cool slightly.

5. Beat confectioners' sugar, butter, vanilla and enough milk to reach a drizzling consistency. Drizzle icing over warm rolls.

1 CINNAMON ROLL: 429 cal., 10g fat (6g sat. fat), 16mg chol., 311mg sod., 81g carb. (48g sugars, 1g fiber), 5g pro.

English Marmalade Pecan Bread

My dad had a very British upbringing and, boy, did he love his marmalade! When I baked the jam into this nutty bread, everyone loved it—even my kids.
—*Nancy Heishman, Las Vegas, NV*

PREP: 20 MIN. • **BAKE:** 50 MIN. + COOLING • **MAKES:** 1 LOAF (16 SLICES)

½ **cup butter, softened**
½ **cup packed brown sugar**
2 **large eggs, room temperature**
1 **jar (10 oz.) orange marmalade spreadable fruit**
2⅔ **cups all-purpose flour**
3 **tsp. baking powder**
2 **tsp. ground cinnamon**
1 **tsp. salt**
⅓ **cup orange juice**
½ **cup chopped pecans**

1. Preheat oven to 350°. Grease and flour a 9x5-in. loaf pan. In a large bowl, beat butter and brown sugar until blended. Add eggs, 1 at a time, beating well after each addition. Gradually beat in marmalade. In another bowl, whisk flour, baking powder, cinnamon and salt; add to butter mixture alternately with orange juice, beating well after each addition. Fold in pecans.

2. Transfer to prepared pan. Bake 50-60 minutes or until a toothpick inserted in center comes out clean. Cool in pan 10 minutes before removing to a wire rack to cool.

FREEZE OPTION: Securely wrap cooled loaf in plastic and foil. To use, thaw wrapped loaf at room temperature. If desired, warm slices in toaster or microwave.

1 SLICE: 226 cal., 9g fat (4g sat. fat), 39mg chol., 132mg sod., 33g carb. (15g sugars, 1g fiber), 3g pro.

Lovin' Spoolful

Create this pretty plaque that's also a key holder.

WHAT YOU'LL NEED
Unfinished wood craft plaque
Vintage wood thread spools
Heart pattern
Pink acrylic craft paint
2 sponge brushes
3 decorative skeleton keys
Silver ball keychain
Silver heart locket
Hammer
Nails
Glue gun
Faux metal key lock plate
   and brad nails, optional

DIRECTIONS
1. Dip a sponge brush into paint, then into water. Apply a coat to the front and edges of plaque. Work into the wood with dry sponge brush.

2. Cut a paper heart to use as a pattern. Lightly trace heart on front of plaque.

3. Setting one spool aside, arrange spools inside traced heart. Pound a nail through the hole of each. Attach reserved spool to center top of plaque.

4. Erase the traced pencil outline, removing and replacing spools as needed.

5. Glue locket onto spool at top. String keys onto chain. Wrap chain around top spool so keys hang over the center top of heart. If desired, attach lock plate to the center spool of heart with brad nails.

Cream Cheese Raspberry Muffins

These pretty treats are ideal for coffee breaks or to stash in a lunch bag. Bring them to special brunches or simply keep them at home to share with your sweetie.
—*Phyllis Schmalz, Kansas City, KS*

PREP: 25 MIN. • BAKE: 25 MIN. + COOLING • MAKES: 8 MUFFINS

3   oz. cream cheese, softened
2   Tbsp. butter, softened
½   cup sugar
1   large egg, room temperature
1   large egg white, room temperature
3   Tbsp. buttermilk
½   tsp. vanilla extract
¾   cup all-purpose flour
½   tsp. baking powder
⅛   tsp. baking soda
⅛   tsp. salt
¾   cup fresh raspberries
2   Tbsp. chopped walnuts, toasted
¼   cup confectioners' sugar
1   tsp. 2% milk

1. In a small bowl, cream the cream cheese, butter and sugar until smooth. Beat in egg and egg white. Beat in buttermilk and vanilla. Combine the flour, baking powder, baking soda and salt; add to creamed mixture just until moistened. Fold in raspberries and walnuts.

2. Fill 8 paper-lined muffin cups three-fourths full. Bake at 350° for 25-28 minutes or until a toothpick inserted in muffin comes out clean. Cool for 5 minutes before removing from pan to a wire rack to cool completely.

3. Combine the confectioners' sugar and milk; drizzle over the muffins.

1 MUFFIN: 200 cal., 9g fat (4g sat. fat), 46mg chol., 163mg sod., 27g carb. (17g sugars, 1g fiber), 4g pro. **DIABETIC EXCHANGES:** 1 starch, 1 fruit, 1 fat.

Cherry Danish

I won an award when I first made these delicious danishes for a 4-H competition years ago. They're fun change-of-pace valentine snack.
—*Christie Cochran, Canyon, TX*

PREP: 30 MIN. + RISING • **BAKE:** 15 MIN. + COOLING • **MAKES:** 40 SERVINGS

1   pkg. (¼ oz.) active dry yeast
¼   cup warm water (110° to 115°)
1   cup warm 2% milk (110° to 115°)
¾   cup shortening, divided
⅓   cup sugar
3   large eggs, room temperature, divided use
1   tsp. salt
¼   tsp. each ground mace, lemon extract and vanilla extract
4   to 4½ cups all-purpose flour
1   can (21 oz.) cherry pie filling

GLAZE
1½   cups confectioners' sugar
½   tsp. vanilla extract
2   to 3 Tbsp. whole milk
⅓   cup chopped almonds

1. In a large bowl, dissolve yeast in water. Add the milk, ¼ cup shortening, sugar, 2 eggs, salt, mace, extracts and 2 cups of flour; beat until smooth. Add enough remaining flour to form a soft dough.

2. Turn onto a floured surface; knead until smooth and elastic, 6-8 minutes. Place in a greased bowl, turning once to grease top. Cover and let rise in a warm place until doubled, about 1 hour.

3. Punch dough down. On a large floured surface, roll dough out to a 24x16-in. rectangle. Dot half of the dough with ¼ cup shortening; fold dough lengthwise. Fold the dough 3 times lengthwise, then 2 times widthwise, each time dotting with some of the remaining shortening. Place dough in a greased bowl; cover and let rise 20 minutes.

4. On a floured surface, roll dough into a 16x15-in. rectangle. Cut into 8x¾-in. strips; coil into spiral shapes, tucking ends underneath. Place in 2 greased 15x10x1-in. baking pans. Cover and let rise in a warm place until doubled, about 1 hour.

5. Beat remaining egg. Make a depression in the center of each roll; brush with egg. Fill with 1 Tbsp. pie filling. Bake at 375° for 15-18 minutes or until golden brown. Cool on a wire rack. Combine the first 3 glaze ingredients; drizzle over rolls. Sprinkle with almonds.

1 PASTRY: 137 cal., 5g fat (1g sat. fat), 17mg chol., 70mg sod., 21g carb. (10g sugars, 1g fiber), 2g pro.

Lemon Pound Cake Muffins

I make these lemony muffins for all kinds of occasions. My family is always asking for them. They have a rich cakelike texture and a sweet, tangy flavor.

—Lola Baxter, Winnebago, MN

PREP: 15 MIN. • BAKE: 20 MIN. • MAKES: 1 DOZEN

½ cup butter, softened
1 cup sugar
2 large eggs, room temperature
½ cup sour cream
1 tsp. vanilla extract
½ tsp. lemon extract
1¾ cups all-purpose flour
½ tsp. salt
¼ tsp. baking soda

GLAZE
2 cups confectioners' sugar
3 Tbsp. lemon juice

1. In a large bowl, cream the butter and sugar until light and fluffy, 5-7 minutes. Add eggs, 1 at a time, beating well after each addition. Beat in the sour cream and extracts. Combine the flour, salt and baking soda; add to creamed mixture just until moistened.

2. Fill 12 greased or paper-lined muffin cups three-fourths full. Bake at 400° until a toothpick inserted in the center comes out clean, 18-20 minutes. Cool for 5 minutes before removing from pan to a wire rack.

3. Combine the glaze ingredients; drizzle over muffins. Serve warm.

1 MUFFIN: 311 cal., 10g fat (6g sat. fat), 63mg chol., 218mg sod., 51g carb. (36g sugars, 1g fiber), 3g pro.

READER REVIEW
"These are so easy and tasty! I added lemon zest for a little more zing but they are a stand-alone act. They are wonderful even without the glaze. They come out tender and moist. I used Greek plain yogurt instead of sour cream. I am sure they'd be wonderful with orange flavors, too."
—JON.RUTH.ALUMBAUGH, TASTEOFHOME.COM

One-Bowl Chocolate Chip Bread

My family of chocoholics hops out of bed on Valentine's Day because they know I'm baking this indulgent quick bread for breakfast. But don't wait for a special occasion to enjoy it!
—*Angela Lively, Conroe, TX*

PREP: 20 MIN. • BAKE: 65 MINUTES • MAKES: 1 LOAF (16 SLICES)

3 **large eggs, room temperature**
1 **cup sugar**
2 **cups sour cream**
3 **cups self-rising flour**
2 **cups semisweet chocolate chips**

1. Preheat oven to 350°. Beat eggs, sugar and sour cream until well blended. Gradually stir in flour. Fold in chocolate chips. Transfer to a greased 9x5-in. loaf pan.

2. Bake until a toothpick comes out clean, 65-75 minutes. Cool in pan 5 minutes before removing to a wire rack to cool completely.

1 SLICE: 306 cal., 13g fat (8g sat. fat), 42mg chol., 305mg sod., 44g carb. (25g sugars, 2g fiber), 5g pro.

Sweetheart Cornbread

This is a delicious recipe I've served many times to my family. I don't always shape the bread into a heart, but it is fun to do that for Valentine's Day or another special occasion. Even if you don't have a heart-shaped pan, garnishing with ribbon adds a colorful touch.
—*Dottie Miller, Jonesborough, TN*

PREP: 10 MIN. • BAKE: 20 MIN. + COOLING • MAKES: 8 SERVINGS

2 **large eggs, room temperature**
1 **cup sour cream**
½ **cup canola oil**
1 **can (8¼ oz.) cream-style corn**
1½ **cups cornmeal**
¼ **cup all-purpose flour**
2¼ **tsp. baking powder**
¾ **tsp. salt**

In a large bowl, beat the eggs. Add sour cream, oil and corn; mix well. Stir in the dry ingredients just until combined. Pour into a greased and floured 5-cup heart shaped baking pan or a 9-in. round pan. Bake at 425° for 20-25 minutes or until a toothpick comes out clean. Cool 10 minutes in pan before removing to a wire rack.

1 PIECE: 328 cal., 20g fat (6g sat. fat), 73mg chol., 446mg sod., 29g carb. (2g sugars, 2g fiber), 6g pro.

Blueberry Sour Cream Coffee Cake

At our house, special breakfasts would not be the same without this delicious coffee cake. Folks rave about the treat when I bring it to holiday celebrations.
—*Susan Walschlager, Anderson, IN*

PREP: 25 MIN. • **BAKE:** 55 MIN. + COOLING • **MAKES:** 12 SERVINGS

¾ cup butter, softened
1½ cups sugar
4 large eggs, room temperature
1 tsp. vanilla extract
3 cups all-purpose flour
1½ tsp. baking powder
¾ tsp. baking soda
¼ tsp. salt
1 cup sour cream

FILLING
¼ cup packed brown sugar
1 Tbsp. all-purpose flour
½ tsp. ground cinnamon
2 cups fresh or frozen blueberries

GLAZE
1 cup confectioners' sugar
2 to 3 Tbsp. 2% milk

1. Preheat oven to 350°. In a large bowl, cream butter and sugar until light and fluffy, 5-7 minutes. Add eggs, 1 at a time, beating well after each addition. Beat in vanilla. Combine the flour, baking powder, baking soda and salt; add to creamed mixture alternately with sour cream, beating well after each addition.

2. Spoon a third of the batter into a greased and floured 10-in. fluted tube pan. Combine brown sugar, flour and cinnamon; sprinkle half over batter. Top with half of the berries. Repeat layers. Top with remaining batter.

3. Bake 55-65 minutes or until a toothpick inserted in the center comes out clean. Cool 10 minutes before removing from pan to a wire rack to cool completely. Combine glaze ingredients; drizzle over coffee cake.

1 PIECE: 448 cal., 17g fat (10g sat. fat), 114mg chol., 328mg sod., 68g carb. (42g sugars, 1g fiber), 6g pro.

NOTES

Heart's Desire Pizza

Sweethearts of all ages will have a delightful time sprinkling these fun personal pizzas with whatever tasty toppings they love most. The pizzas are ideal for parties with friends, too!
—Taste of Home *Test Kitchen*

PREP: 25 MIN. • **BAKE:** 10 MIN. • **MAKES:** 8 INDIVIDUAL PIZZAS

1 tube (16.3 oz.) large refrigerated flaky biscuits
1 jar (14 oz.) pizza sauce
Optional toppings: sliced ripe olives, sliced and quartered pepperoni, chopped fresh mushrooms, chopped green and sweet yellow pepper
1½ cups shredded mozzarella cheese
1½ cups shredded cheddar cheese

Cut eight 6-in.-square pieces of aluminum foil; place on baking sheets. Lightly coat foil with cooking spray; set aside. On a lightly floured surface, roll each biscuit to a 5-in. square. Cut a 1-in. triangle from the center top and place on the center bottom, forming a heart. Press edges to seal. Transfer to foil squares. Spoon pizza sauce over dough to within ¼ in. of edges. If desired, sprinkle with toppings. Top with cheeses. Bake at 425° for 10-15 minutes or until golden brown.

1 PIZZA: 342 cal., 19g fat (9g sat. fat), 38mg chol., 925mg sod., 30g carb. (7g sugars, 2g fiber), 13g pro.

PERFECT PAIRING
Hosting a pizza party? Choose a food-friendly Italian red wine such as Chianti, barbera or montepulciano. These wines are all easygoing, light and perfect for a fun night of pizza! Chianti has the most palate-cleansing tannins, great if you like lots of rich, meaty toppings. Barbera is the most light-bodied and juicy of the three, and crowd-pleasing montepulciano lands in the middle.

Spinach & Feta Stuffed Chicken

My chicken bundles are simple and comforting, yet feel extra special.
Serve them with a quick rice pilaf for a perfect meal for two.
—*Jim Knepper, Mount Holly Springs, PA*

TAKES: 30 MIN. • MAKES: 2 SERVINGS

8   oz. fresh spinach
    (about 10 cups)
1½ tsp. cider vinegar
½   tsp. sugar
⅛   tsp. pepper
2   boneless skinless
    chicken thighs
½   tsp. chicken seasoning
3   Tbsp. crumbled
    feta cheese
1   tsp. olive oil
¾   cup reduced-sodium
    chicken broth
1   tsp. butter

1. Preheat oven to 375°. In a large skillet, cook and stir spinach over medium-high heat until wilted. Stir in the vinegar, sugar and pepper; cool slightly.

2. Pound the chicken thighs with a meat mallet to flatten slightly; sprinkle with chicken seasoning. Top chicken with spinach mixture and cheese. Roll up chicken from a long side; tie securely with kitchen string.

3. In an ovenproof skillet, heat oil over medium-high heat; add the chicken and brown on all sides. Transfer to oven; roast until a thermometer inserted in chicken reads 170°, 13-15 minutes.

4. Remove chicken from pan; keep warm. On stovetop, add broth and butter to skillet; bring to a boil, stirring to loosen browned bits from pan. Cook until pan sauce is slightly thickened, 3-5 minutes. Serve with chicken.

1 CHICKEN ROLL-UP WITH 2 TBSP. SAUCE: 253 cal., 14g fat (5g sat. fat), 86mg chol., 601mg sod., 5g carb. (2g sugars, 2g fiber), 26g pro. **DIABETIC EXCHANGES:** 3 lean meat, 2 vegetable, 1½ fat.

Garlic Lemon Shrimp

This shrimp dish is amazingly quick to get on the table. Serve it with crusty bread
so you can soak up all of the luscious garlic lemon sauce.
—*Athena Russell, Greenville, SC*

TAKES: 20 MIN. • MAKES: 4 SERVINGS

2 Tbsp. olive oil
1 lb. uncooked shrimp
   (26-30 per lb.), peeled
   and deveined
3 garlic cloves,
   thinly sliced
1 Tbsp. lemon juice
1 tsp. ground cumin
¼ tsp. salt
2 Tbsp. minced fresh
   parsley
   Hot cooked pasta
   or rice

In a large skillet, heat oil over medium-high heat; saute
shrimp 3 minutes. Add garlic, lemon juice, cumin and salt;
cook and stir until shrimp turn pink. Stir in parsley. Serve
with pasta.

1 SERVING: 163 cal., 8g fat (1g sat. fat), 138mg chol.,
284mg sod., 2g carb. (0 sugars, 0 fiber), 19g pro.
DIABETIC EXCHANGES: 3 lean meat, 1½ fat.

Spice-Rubbed Lamb Chops

One of my absolute favorite meals to eat anytime are lamb chops! My daughters love
watching me make my delicious chops, but they love eating them even more!
—*Nareman Dietz, Beverly Hills, MI*

PREP: 15 MIN. + CHILLING • BAKE: 5 MIN. • MAKES: 2 SERVINGS

2 tsp. lemon juice
2 tsp. Worcestershire
   sauce
1½ tsp. pepper
1¼ tsp. ground cumin
1¼ tsp. curry powder
1 garlic clove, minced
½ tsp. sea salt
½ tsp. onion powder
½ tsp. crushed red
   pepper flakes
4 lamb rib chops
1 Tbsp. olive oil

1. Mix first 9 ingredients; spread over chops. Refrigerate,
covered, overnight.

2. Preheat oven to 450°. In an ovenproof skillet, heat oil
over medium high heat; brown chops, about 2 minutes
per side. Transfer to oven; roast until desired doneness
(for medium-rare, a thermometer should read 135°;
medium, 140°), 3-4 minutes.

2 LAMB CHOPS: 290 cal., 17g fat (4g sat. fat), 90mg chol.,
620mg sod., 5g carb. (1g sugars, 2g fiber), 29g pro.
DIABETIC EXCHANGES: 4 lean meat, 1½ fat.

Lobster alla Diavola

I've cooked lobster alla diavola (devil's style) since I was first married. We serve lobster during special holidays, usually with linguine or capellini.
—*Marcia Whitney, Gainesville, FL*

PREP: 20 MIN. • **COOK:** 35 MIN. • **MAKES:** 6 SERVINGS

6   fresh or frozen lobster tails (4 to 5 oz. each), thawed
3   Tbsp. olive oil
1   jalapeno pepper, seeded and minced
3   garlic cloves, minced
1   can (28 oz.) whole plum tomatoes, undrained
½   cup julienned soft sun-dried tomatoes (not packed in oil)
½   cup dry red wine
1   tsp. sugar
2   tsp. salt-free Italian herb seasoning
½   tsp. smoked paprika, optional
¼   tsp. salt
⅛   tsp. pepper
1   Tbsp. red wine vinegar
2   Tbsp. butter
3   Tbsp. finely chopped shallots
   Hot cooked linguine and minced fresh parsley

1. Using kitchen scissors, cut through bottom of lobster tail lengthwise down the center. Place lobster tail, cut side up, on a cutting board. Using a chef's knife, cut through lobster meat and shell. Carefully remove meat from shell and cut into 1-in. pieces. Set lobster shells aside.

2. In a 6-qt. stockpot, heat oil over medium-high heat. Add jalapeno; cook and stir 1-2 minutes or until tender. Add garlic; cook 1 minute longer.

3. Add tomatoes, dried tomatoes, wine, sugar and seasonings, breaking up tomatoes with a spoon. Add reserved lobster shells. Bring to a boil. Reduce heat; simmer, covered, 25-30 minutes, stirring occasionally. Remove shells; set aside. Stir in vinegar.

4. In a large skillet, heat butter over medium-high heat. Add shallots; cook and stir until tender. Add lobster meat; cook and stir 2-4 minutes or until meat is opaque. Stir into tomato mixture. Bring to a boil. Reduce heat; simmer, uncovered, 2-3 minutes or until meat is firm but tender.

5. To serve, fill lobster shells with tomato mixture. Serve with linguine; sprinkle with parsley.

1 SERVING: 254 cal., 11g fat (4g sat. fat), 154mg chol., 820mg sod., 12g carb. (7g sugars, 4g fiber), 20g pro.

Sweet Stack

Turn wood slices in to mini valentines that can be used to adorn a vase of flowers, hang from a doorknob or spruce up cabinet pulls. Or glue a magnet to the back for an adorable refrigerator magnet that's sure to bring a smile.

You can also create clever name tags for gifts any time of the year. Just change up the paint colors.

DIRECTIONS

1. For each valentine, use a flat brush and regular or outdoor acrylic craft paint to paint a solid purple or fuchsia circle on front of the wood slice to within about ¼ in. of edge. Let dry.

2. Add coats as needed until paint is bright, letting dry after each coat. Paint a solid heart in center or use a paint pen to write a message.

3. If you'd like, make a pattern of dots around the design or add other artistic embellishments using the paint pen or the end of a liner brush.

4. Drill a hole through each wood slice about ½ in. below the top edge. Thread a 14-in. length of jute twine through each hole. Secure the loop with a knot.

Herb-Crusted Prime Rib

Prime rib always makes an impression and it's actually easy to prepare.
This roast is wonderfully flavored with lots of fresh herbs.
—*Jennifer Dennis, Alhambra, CA*

PREP: 20 MIN. • BAKE: 1¾ HOURS + STANDING • MAKES: 8 SERVINGS

1 **large shallot, coarsely chopped**
6 **garlic cloves, quartered**
3 **Tbsp. minced fresh rosemary or 1 Tbsp. dried rosemary**
2 **Tbsp. minced fresh oregano or 2 tsp. dried oregano**
2 **Tbsp. minced fresh thyme or 2 tsp. dried thyme**
2 **Tbsp. minced fresh sage or 2 tsp. rubbed sage**
2 **Tbsp. olive oil**
3 **tsp. pepper**
1 **tsp. salt**
1 **bone-in beef rib roast (4 lbs.)**

SAUCE
1½ **cups reduced-sodium beef broth**
1 **cup dry red wine or additional reduced-sodium beef broth**
1 **tsp. butter**
½ **tsp. salt**

1. Preheat oven to 350°. Place the first 6 ingredients in a food processor; cover and pulse until finely chopped. Add oil, pepper and salt; cover and process until blended. Rub over roast. Place on a rack in a large roasting pan.

2. Bake, uncovered, 1¾-2¼ hours or until meat reaches desired doneness (for medium-rare, a thermometer should read 135°; medium, 140°; medium-well, 145°).

3. Remove roast to a serving platter and keep warm; let stand 15 minutes before slicing.

4. Meanwhile, in a small saucepan, bring broth and wine to a boil; cook until liquid is reduced to 1 cup. Remove from heat; stir in butter and salt. Slice roast; serve with sauce.

8 OZ.: 338 cal., 19g fat (7g sat. fat), 92mg chol., 612mg sod., 4g carb. (1g sugars, 0 fiber), 31g pro.

A MUST-TRY MATCH
Pair this prime rib with a Bordeaux blend from California. Inspired by the wines of Bordeaux, France, winemakers blend cabernet, merlot and up to three other grapes to create this lush, rich red wine that's delicious with beef.

Wild Rice-Stuffed Pork Loin

This recipe features wild rice and apricot stuffing tucked inside a tender pork roast. It's the perfect entree when you want to surprise a special someone.
—*Kim Rubner, Worthington, IA*

PREP: 20 MIN. • **BAKE:** 1½ HOURS + STANDING • **MAKES:** 10 SERVINGS

1 whole boneless pork loin roast (4 lbs.), trimmed
1 tsp. salt
½ tsp. garlic powder
¼ tsp. pepper
2 cups wild rice, cooked and drained
1½ cups coarsely chopped dried apricots
1 cup chopped onion
¾ cup finely chopped celery
¾ cup minced fresh parsley
½ tsp. rubbed sage
½ tsp. dried thyme
½ cup chicken broth
10 bacon strips
   Apricot preserves, optional

1. To butterfly pork roast, cut a lengthwise slit down the center of the pork loin to within ½ in. of bottom. Open loin so it lies flat. On each half, make another lengthwise slit down the center to within ½ in. of bottom. Flatten to ¼-in. thickness.

2. Sprinkle with salt, garlic powder and pepper.

3. In a large bowl, combine rice, apricots, onion, celery, parsley, sage, thyme and broth. Spread stuffing evenly over pork, ¼-½ in. thick. Roll up jelly-roll style, starting with a long side. Tie the roast at 1½-2-in. intervals with kitchen string. Place the remaining stuffing in a greased shallow 2-qt. baking dish; set aside.

4. Bake roast, uncovered, at 350° 1 hour. Remove roast from oven; carefully remove string. Place bacon strips over top of roast, overlapping slightly. Bake until the bacon is browned and crisp and a thermometer reads 160°, 30-45 minutes longer. If needed, broil 4 in. from heat until bacon reaches desired crispness. Meanwhile, cover and bake remaining stuffing until heated through, about 30 minutes.

5. Let roast stand for 10 minutes before slicing. If desired, brush with apricot preserves before slicing.

1 SERVING: 436 cal., 20g fat (7g sat. fat), 109mg chol., 547mg sod., 23g carb. (10g sugars, 3g fiber), 41g pro.

Garlic Clove Chicken

My neighbors made this chicken frequently, and I couldn't get enough of it.
If you like garlic, you'll love this recipe.
—Denise Hollebeke, Penhold, AB

PREP: 10 MIN. • **BAKE:** 2¼ HOURS + STANDING • **MAKES:** 6 SERVINGS

1 roasting chicken
  (5 to 6 lbs.)
1 small onion, quartered
40 garlic cloves, peeled
¼ cup canola oil
1½ tsp. salt
1 tsp. dried parsley
  flakes
½ tsp. dried celery flakes
½ tsp. each dried
  tarragon, thyme and
  rosemary, crushed
¼ tsp. pepper

1. Place chicken breast side up on a rack in a shallow roasting pan. Stuff onion in chicken and tie drumsticks together. Arrange garlic cloves around chicken. In a small bowl, combine the remaining ingredients. Drizzle over chicken and garlic.

2. Cover and bake at 350° for 1¾ hours. Uncover; bake 30-45 minutes longer or until a thermometer inserted in thickest part of thigh reads 170°-175°, basting occasionally with the pan drippings. (Cover loosely with foil if chicken browns too quickly.) Cover and let stand for 10 minutes before slicing.

7 OZ. COOKED CHICKEN: 556 cal., 36g fat (8g sat. fat), 149mg chol., 738mg sod., 8g carb. (1g sugars, 1g fiber), 49g pro.

READER REVIEW
"I recently made this chicken, and my hubby and I really enjoyed it. Nice change from the way I usually make a lot of my chicken dishes."
—NANAOF11, TASTEOFHOME.COM

Crown Roast with Apricot Dressing

I've been making crown roasts for years but was only satisfied with the results when I combined recipes to come up with this guest-pleasing version.
—*Isabell Cooper, Cambridge, NS*

PREP: 20 MIN. • **BAKE:** 2½ HOURS + STANDING • **MAKES:** 12 SERVINGS

1   **pork crown roast (12 ribs and about 8 lbs.)**
½   **tsp. seasoned salt**
⅓   **cup apricot preserves**

APRICOT DRESSING
¼   **cup butter, cubed**
1   **cup sliced fresh mushrooms**
1   **medium onion, finely chopped**
1   **celery rib, finely chopped**
1   **cup chopped dried apricots**
½   **tsp. dried savory**
½   **tsp. dried thyme**
¼   **tsp. salt**
¼   **tsp. pepper**
3   **cups soft bread crumbs**

1. Preheat oven to 350°. Place crown roast on a rack in a shallow roasting pan. Sprinkle with seasoned salt. Bake, uncovered, 1 hour.

2. Brush sides of the roast with preserves. Bake until a thermometer reads 145°, 1½-2 hours longer. Carefully transfer roast to a serving platter. Let stand 20 minutes before carving.

3. For the dressing, in a large skillet, heat butter over medium-high heat. Add mushrooms, onion and celery; cook and stir 6-8 minutes or until tender. Stir in apricots and seasonings. Add bread crumbs; toss to coat. Transfer to a greased 8-in. square baking dish. Bake 15-20 minutes or until lightly browned. Carve roast between ribs; serve with the dressing.

1 RIB WITH ⅓ CUP STUFFING: 419 cal., 19g fat (8g sat. fat), 105mg chol., 293mg sod., 20g carb. (10g sugars, 1g fiber), 40g pro.

A BOTTLE OF BUBBLY
Consider enjoying a bottle of sparkling Asti Spumante with this roast. Bubbles make everything better, and this spritzy, lightly sweet charmer sets a festive tone.

Beef Filets with Portobello Sauce

These tasty steaks seem special but they are fast enough for a weeknight schedule. Try it with crusty French bread, mixed salad and a light lemon dessert.
—*Christel Stein, Tampa, FL*

TAKES: 20 MIN. • **MAKES:** 2 SERVINGS

2 beef tenderloin steaks (4 oz. each)
1¾ cups sliced baby portobello mushrooms (about 4 oz.)
½ cup dry red wine or reduced-sodium beef broth
1 tsp. all-purpose flour
½ cup reduced-sodium beef broth
1 tsp. ketchup
1 tsp. steak sauce
1 tsp. Worcestershire sauce
½ tsp. ground mustard
¼ tsp. pepper
⅛ tsp. salt
1 Tbsp. minced fresh chives, optional

1. Place a large skillet coated with cooking spray over medium-high heat; brown steaks on both sides. Remove from pan.

2. Add the mushrooms and wine to pan; bring to a boil over medium heat, stirring to loosen browned bits from pan. Cook until liquid is reduced by half, 2-3 minutes. Mix flour and broth until smooth; stir into pan. Stir in all remaining ingredients except chives; bring to a boil.

3. Return the steaks to pan; cook, uncovered, until meat reaches desired doneness (for medium-rare, a thermometer should read 135°; medium, 140°), 1-2 minutes per side. If desired, sprinkle with chives.

1 STEAK WITH ⅓ CUP SAUCE: 247 cal., 7g fat (3g sat. fat), 51mg chol., 369mg sod., 7g carb. (3g sugars, 1g fiber), 27g pro. **DIABETIC EXCHANGES:** 3 lean meat, 1 vegetable.

READER REVIEW
"I made this for our Valentines dinner. Delicious and easy!"
—AORLA846, TASTEOFHOME.COM

CHAPTER 7

Love You to Pieces

Raspberry Cake

Jazz up a plain sheet cake with raspberry gelatin and frozen berries. Spread with a light, fruity whipped topping, it makes a cool and refreshing dessert.
—*Marion Anderson, Dalton, MN*

PREP: 10 MIN. + CHILLING • BAKE: 35 MIN. + COOLING • MAKES: 16 SERVINGS

1   pkg. white cake mix
    (regular size)
1   pkg. (3 oz.) raspberry
    gelatin
4   large eggs
½   cup canola oil
¼   cup hot water
1   pkg. (10 oz.)
    frozen sweetened
    raspberries, thawed,
    undrained

FROSTING
1   carton (12 oz.) frozen
    whipped topping,
    thawed
1   pkg. (10 oz.)
    frozen sweetened
    raspberries, thawed,
    undrained
    Fresh raspberries,
    optional

1. In a large bowl, combine the cake mix, gelatin, eggs, oil and water; beat on low speed for 30 seconds. Beat on medium for 2 minutes. Stir in raspberries.

2. Pour into a greased 13x9-in. baking pan. Bake at 350° for 35-40 minutes or until a toothpick inserted in the center comes out clean. Cool.

3. For frosting, in a large bowl, fold whipped topping into raspberries. Spread over cake. Refrigerate for 2 hours before serving. Store in the refrigerator. Garnish with fresh raspberries if desired.

1 PIECE: 330 cal., 15g fat (6g sat. fat), 53mg chol., 233mg sod., 44g carb. (29g sugars, 2g fiber), 4g pro.

NOTES

_____
_____
_____
_____
_____
_____
_____

Bittersweet Chocolate Cheesecake

While it's common for one generation to pass a cherished recipe down to the next, sometimes there's one that's so good it goes the other way! That's the case here: I'm a great-grandmother and I received this recipe from my niece. My entire family enjoys this chocolaty, velvety cheesecake.
—*Amelia Gregory, Omemee, ON*

PREP: 20 MIN. • **BAKE:** 1 HOUR + CHILLING • **MAKES:** 16 SERVINGS

1 cup chocolate wafer crumbs
½ cup finely chopped hazelnuts, toasted
⅓ cup butter, melted
3 pkg. (8 oz. each) cream cheese, softened
1 cup sugar
12 oz. bittersweet chocolate, melted and cooled
1 cup sour cream
1½ tsp. vanilla extract
½ tsp. almond extract
    Dash salt
3 large eggs, room temperature, lightly beaten

GLAZE
4 oz. bittersweet chocolate, chopped
¼ cup heavy whipping cream
1 tsp. vanilla extract
    Optional: Whipped cream and additional toasted hazelnuts

1. Preheat oven to 350°. Mix wafer crumbs, hazelnuts and melted butter; press onto bottom of an ungreased 9-in. springform pan.

2. Beat the cream cheese and sugar until smooth. Beat in cooled chocolate, then sour cream, extracts and salt. Add eggs; beat on low speed just until blended. Pour over crust. Place pan on a baking sheet.

3. Bake until center is almost set, 60-65 minutes. Cool on wire rack 10 minutes. Loosen sides from pan with a knife; cool 1 hour longer. Refrigerate 3 hours.

4. For glaze, in a microwave, melt chocolate with cream; stir until smooth. Stir in vanilla. Spread over chilled cheesecake. Refrigerate, covered, overnight. Remove rim from pan. If desired, served with whipped cream and additional hazelnuts.

1 SLICE: 484 cal., 39g fat (21g sat. fat), 112mg chol., 235mg sod., 34g carb. (24g sugars, 3g fiber), 8g pro.

Mamaw Emily's Strawberry Cake

My husband loved his Mamaw's strawberry cake. He thought no one could duplicate it.
I made it, and it's just as scrumptious as he remembers.
—*Jennifer Bruce, Manitou, KY*

PREP: 15 MIN. • **BAKE:** 25 MIN. + COOLING • **MAKES:** 12 SERVINGS

1 pkg. white cake mix (regular size)
1 pkg. (3 oz.) strawberry gelatin
3 Tbsp. sugar
3 Tbsp. all-purpose flour
1 cup water
½ cup canola oil
2 large eggs, room temperature
1 cup finely chopped strawberries

FROSTING
½ cup butter, softened
½ cup crushed strawberries
4½ to 5 cups confectioners' sugar

1. Preheat oven to 350°. Line bottoms of 2 greased 8-in. round baking pans with parchment; grease parchment.

2. In a large bowl, combine cake mix, gelatin, sugar and flour. Add the water, oil and eggs; beat on low speed for 30 seconds. Beat on medium 2 minutes. Fold in chopped strawberries. Transfer to prepared pans.

3. Bake until a toothpick inserted in center comes out clean, 25-30 minutes. Cool in pans 10 minutes before removing to wire racks; remove paper. Cool completely.

4. For frosting, in a small bowl, beat butter until creamy. Beat in crushed strawberries. Gradually beat in enough confectioners' sugar to reach desired consistency. Spread frosting between layers and over top and sides of cake.

1 SLICE: 532 cal., 21g fat (7g sat. fat), 51mg chol., 340mg sod., 85g carb. (69g sugars, 1g fiber), 4g pro.

READER REVIEW
"This is amazing. Super moist and flavorful. Strawberry buttercream! I'm putting some on my cookies for Valentine's Day!"
—WASOONGU, TASTEOFHOME.COM

Heart's Delight Eclair

This lovely treat is guaranteed to win your sweetie's heart. If you prefer, skip the step of cutting the shape in each pastry sheet and bake them instead as 12-inch squares.
—*Lorene Milligan, Chemainus, BC*

PREP: 30 MIN. + CHILLING • **BAKE:** 15 MIN. • **MAKES:** 12 SERVINGS

1　pkg. (17.3 oz.) frozen puff pastry, thawed
3　cups cold 2% milk
1　pkg. (5.1 oz.) instant vanilla pudding mix
2　cups heavy whipping cream
1　tsp. vanilla extract, divided
1　cup confectioners' sugar
1　Tbsp. water
¼　tsp. almond extract
½　cup semisweet chocolate chips
1　tsp. shortening

1. Preheat oven to 400°. Cut an 11-in. heart-shaped pattern out of parchment or waxed paper.

2. On a lightly floured surface, roll each pastry sheet into a 12-in. square. Using pattern and a sharp knife, cut a heart from each sheet; place on greased baking sheets. Bake until golden brown, 12-15 minutes. Remove to wire racks to cool completely.

3. In a large bowl, whisk the milk and pudding mix for 2 minutes. Let stand until soft-set, about 5 minutes. In another bowl, beat cream and ½ tsp. vanilla until stiff peaks form; lightly fold into pudding.

4. Split each pastry heart into 2 layers; reserve 1 of the top layers. Place 1 of the remaining layers on a serving plate; spread with a third of the pudding mixture. Repeat twice; top with reserved layer.

5. Mix confectioners' sugar, water, almond extract and remaining vanilla until smooth; spread over top pastry.

6. In a microwave, melt chocolate chips and shortening; stir until smooth. Pipe or drizzle over top as desired. Refrigerate until set.

1 PIECE: 488 cal., 29g fat (14g sat. fat), 50mg chol., 252mg sod., 53g carb. (27g sugars, 3g fiber), 6g pro.

Chocolate-Topped Strawberry Cheesecake

Perfect for entertaining, this light and airy cheesecake gets its unique flavor from the chocolate crust. It always brings compliments and adds a touch of elegance to the table.
—*Kathy Berger, Dry Ridge, KY*

PREP: 35 MIN. + CHILLING • **BAKE:** 10 MIN. + COOLING • **MAKES:** 12 SERVINGS

1¼ cups chocolate graham cracker crumbs (about 9 whole crackers)
¼ cup butter, melted
2 envelopes unflavored gelatin
½ cup cold water
16 oz. fresh or frozen unsweetened strawberries, thawed
2 pkg. (8 oz. each) fat-free cream cheese, cubed
1 cup fat-free cottage cheese
Sugar substitute equivalent to ¾ cup sugar
1 carton (8 oz.) frozen reduced-fat whipped topping, thawed, divided
½ cup chocolate ice cream topping
1 cup quartered fresh strawberries

1. Preheat oven to 350°. Mix cracker crumbs and butter; press onto bottom and 1 in. up sides of a 9-in. springform pan coated with cooking spray. Place on a baking sheet. Bake until crust is set, about 10 minutes. Cool completely on a wire rack.

2. In a small saucepan, sprinkle gelatin over cold water; let stand 1 minute. Heat over low heat, stirring until gelatin is completely dissolved; remove from heat.

3. Hull strawberries if necessary; puree berries in a food processor. Remove to a bowl. Add cream cheese, cottage cheese and sugar substitute to food processor; process until smooth. While processing, gradually add the gelatin mixture. Add pureed strawberries; process until blended. Transfer to a large bowl; fold in 2 cups whipped topping. Pour into crust. Refrigerate, covered, until set, 2-3 hours.

4. Loosen sides of cheesecake with a knife; remove rim. To serve, top with chocolate topping, remaining whipped topping and quartered strawberries.

1 SLICE: 244 cal., 8g fat (5g sat. fat), 16mg chol., 463mg sod., 29g carb. (17g sugars, 2g fiber), 10g pro. **DIABETIC EXCHANGES:** 2 starch, 1½ fat.

Lemon Layer Cake

This citrusy cake boasts a flavor duet of sweet and tangy notes. Decorative frosting treatments and edible flowers make it a lovely grand finale to a special occasion dinner.
—*Summer Goddard, Springfield, VA*

PREP: 35 MIN. • **BAKE:** 25 MIN. + COOLING • **MAKES:** 12 SERVINGS

1 cup butter, softened
1½ cups sugar
2 large eggs,
room temperature
3 large egg yolks,
room temperature
1 Tbsp. grated
lemon zest
2 Tbsp. lemon juice
¾ cup sour cream
¼ cup 2% milk
2½ cups all-purpose flour
1 tsp. salt
1 tsp. baking powder
½ tsp. baking soda

SYRUP
½ cup sugar
½ cup lemon juice

FROSTING
2 pkg. (8 oz. each) cream
cheese, softened
1 cup butter, softened
4 cups confectioners'
sugar
1½ tsp. lemon juice
⅛ tsp. salt
Optional: Lemon slices
or edible flowers

1. Preheat oven to 350°. Line bottoms of 2 greased 9-in. round baking pans with parchment; grease parchment.

2. Cream the butter and sugar until light and fluffy, 5-7 minutes. Add eggs and egg yolks, 1 at a time, beating well after each addition. Beat in lemon zest and juice. In a small bowl, mix the sour cream and milk. In another bowl, whisk together flour, salt, baking powder and baking soda; add to creamed mixture alternately with sour cream mixture.

3. Transfer batter to prepared pans. Bake until a toothpick inserted in center comes out clean, 24-28 minutes. Cool in pans 10 minutes before removing to wire racks; remove parchment. Cool slightly.

4. For syrup, in a small saucepan, combine the sugar and lemon juice. Bring to a boil; cook until liquid is reduced by half. Cool completely.

5. For frosting, beat softened cream cheese and butter until smooth; beat in the confectioners' sugar, lemon juice and salt until blended.

6. Using a long serrated knife, cut each cake horizontally in half. Brush layers with warm syrup; cool completely.

7. Place 1 cake layer on a serving plate; spread with 1 cup frosting. Repeat layers twice. Top with the remaining cake layer. Frost the top and sides of cake with the remaining frosting. If desired, top with lemon slices or edible flowers. Refrigerate leftovers.

1 SLICE: 841 cal., 48g fat (30g sat. fat), 219mg chol., 656mg sod., 96g carb. (72g sugars, 1g fiber), 8g pro.

Chocolate Tart with Cranberry Raspberry Sauce

With its rich chocolate and fruit flavors, a small piece of this tart goes a long way.
If you want to make this even more special, top it with whipped cream.
—Diane Nemitz, Ludington, MI

PREP: 40 MIN. • BAKE: 40 MIN. + COOLING • MAKES: 12 SERVINGS

1 cup all-purpose flour
½ cup old-fashioned oats
¼ cup sugar
½ cup cold butter, cubed
1½ cups unblanched almonds
½ cup packed brown sugar
½ cup dark corn syrup
2 large eggs, room temperature
4 oz. bittersweet chocolate, melted
2 Tbsp. butter, melted

SAUCE
2 cups fresh raspberries, divided
1 cup fresh or frozen cranberries, thawed
¾ cup sugar
2 Tbsp. port wine or water

1. Preheat oven to 350°. Process flour, oats and sugar in a food processor until oats are ground. Add butter; pulse until crumbly. Press onto bottom and 1 in. up sides of an ungreased 10-in. springform pan. Bake until lightly browned, 14-16 minutes. Cool on a wire rack.

2. Process almonds in a food processor until coarsely chopped. Beat brown sugar, corn syrup, eggs, chocolate and melted butter; stir in almonds.

3. Pour into prepared crust. Bake until center is set and crust is golden brown, 25-30 minutes. Cool completely on a wire rack.

4. Meanwhile, in a small saucepan, combine 1 cup fresh raspberries, cranberries, sugar and wine. Bring to a boil, stirring to dissolve the sugar. Reduce heat to low; cook, uncovered, until cranberries pop, 4-5 minutes, stirring occasionally. Remove from heat; cool slightly.

5. Press berry mixture through a fine-mesh strainer into a bowl; discard seeds. Refrigerate sauce until serving.

6. Remove rim from pan. Serve tart with sauce and remaining raspberries.

1 SLICE WITH 4 TSP. SAUCE: 462 cal., 24g fat (9g sat. fat), 56mg chol., 115mg sod., 55g carb. (39g sugars, 4g fiber), 7g pro.

Easy Pink Lemonade Pie

Pucker up, buttercup! Here's an easy no-bake pink pie perfect for a romantic holiday. A saltine crust is amazing with a tart-sweet strawberry lemonade filling. The best part is it doesn't require that you spend all day in the kitchen.

—*Gina Nistico, Denver, CO*

PREP: 30 MIN. + CHILLING • **BAKE:** 15 MIN. + COOLING • **MAKES:** 8 SERVINGS

2¾ cups coarsely
   crushed saltines
   (about 60 crackers)
1 cup sugar, divided
½ cup butter, melted
2 cups sliced fresh
   or frozen sliced
   strawberries, thawed
1 tsp. lemon juice
1 tsp. grated lemon zest
¼ cup cold water
1 envelope unflavored
   gelatin
2 pkg. (8 oz. each) cream
   cheese, softened
½ cup heavy whipping
   cream
   Lemon slices, optional

1. Preheat oven to 350°. Combine the crushed crackers and ¼ cup sugar with melted butter. Using the bottom of a glass, press cracker mixture onto bottom and up the sides of a greased 9-in. deep-dish pie plate. Bake until set, 15-18 minutes. Cool completely on a wire rack.

2. Combine strawberries, ½ cup sugar, lemon juice and zest; let stand 10 minutes. Meanwhile, sprinkle gelatin over cold water; let stand 5 minutes. Transfer strawberry mixture to a food processor or blender; pulse until mixture is smooth. Microwave gelatin on high until melted, about 10 seconds; stir into strawberry mixture.

3. Beat cream cheese and remaining sugar until smooth. Gradually beat in cream and strawberry mixture. Transfer filling to crust. Refrigerate pie, covered, until set, about 2 hours. If desired, top with lemon slices.

1 PIECE: 566 cal., 39g fat (23g sat. fat), 105mg chol., 502mg sod., 50g carb. (30g sugars, 2g fiber), 7g pro.

READER REVIEW
"The crust made from saltines turned out so easy and nice. I added a bit more lemon, just because I like it. This was quick and it looks nice. I may garnish with fresh berries—but it is great just as is."
—MISSCOFFEEPOT, TASTEOFHOME.COM

Favorite Coconut Cake

When I need an impressive dessert for a special occasion, this is the recipe I depend on. My guests are glad I do! Add heart-shaped sprinkles to dress it up for Valentine's Day.
—*Edna Hoffman, Hebron, IN*

PREP: 45 MIN. • **BAKE:** 15 MIN. + COOLING • **MAKES:** 16 SERVINGS

4 **large egg whites**
¾ **cup butter, softened**
1½ **cups sugar, divided**
1 **tsp. almond extract**
1 **tsp. vanilla extract**
2¾ **cups cake flour**
4 **tsp. baking powder**
¾ **tsp. salt**
1 **cup whole milk**

FROSTING
5 **large egg whites**
1⅔ **cups sugar**
1 **Tbsp. water**
½ **tsp. cream of tartar**
1 **tsp. vanilla extract**
2½ **cups unsweetened coconut flakes**
Colored sprinkles, optional

1. Place 4 egg whites in a large bowl; let stand at room temperature 30 minutes. Line bottoms of 3 greased 9-in. round baking pans with parchment; grease parchment. Preheat oven to 350°.

2. Cream butter and 1 cup sugar until light and fluffy, 5-7 minutes; beat in extracts. In another bowl, whisk together flour, baking powder and salt; add to creamed mixture alternately with milk.

3. With clean beaters, beat egg whites on medium speed until soft peaks form. Gradually add the remaining sugar, 1 Tbsp. at a time, beating on high after each addition until sugar is dissolved. Continue beating until stiff glossy peaks form. Fold into batter.

4. Transfer batter to prepared pans. Bake until a toothpick inserted in center comes out clean, 13-17 minutes. Cool in pans 10 minutes before removing to wire racks; remove paper. Cool completely.

5. For frosting, in a large heatproof bowl, whisk egg whites, sugar, water and cream of tartar until blended. Place over simmering water in a large saucepan over medium heat; whisking constantly, heat mixture until a thermometer reads 160°, 2-3 minutes. Remove from heat; add vanilla. Beat on high speed until stiff glossy peaks form, about 7 minutes.

6. Spread between layers and over top and sides of cake. Cover with coconut. If desired, decorate with sprinkles. Store, uncovered, in refrigerator.

1 SLICE: 400 cal., 16g fat (11g sat. fat), 24mg chol., 341mg sod., 62g carb. (41g sugars, 2g fiber), 5g pro.

Conversation Cupcakes

It's a snap to spell out sweet sentiments on these quaint cupcakes when you bake a batch ahead of time using convenient cake mix. You don't even need a heart-shaped muffin tin to make them.
—Taste of Home *Test Kitchen*

PREP: 45 MIN. • BAKE: 20 MIN. + COOLING • MAKES: 28 CUPCAKES

1 **pkg. white cake mix (regular size)**
½ **cup butter, softened**
½ **cup shortening**
2 **Tbsp. 2% milk**
1 **tsp. vanilla extract**
⅛ **tsp. butter flavoring, optional**
4 **cups confectioners' sugar**
   Assorted food coloring, optional

1. Preheat oven to 350°. Line muffin cups with foil or paper liners. Prepare the cake mix batter according to package directions for cupcakes. Place 1 marble (or marble-sized foil ball) in each muffin cup between liners and muffin pan to create heart shape.

2. Fill prepared cups half full. Bake according to package directions for cupcakes. Cool in pans 10 minutes before removing to wire racks to cool completely.

3. For frosting, in a large bowl, beat butter, shortening, milk, vanilla and, if desired, butter flavoring until smooth. Gradually beat in confectioners' sugar. If desired, tint frosting with food coloring. Frost cupcakes and decorate with Valentine messages.

1 CUPCAKE: 228 cal., 11g fat (4g sat. fat), 29mg chol., 163mg sod., 32g carb. (24g sugars, 0 fiber), 2g pro.

NOTES

Gooey Chocolate-Peanut Bars

These are so easy to make and take no time at all. They're great to package up for those college kids looking for something from home. Everyone will want this recipe.
—*Elaine Grimme, Sioux Falls, SD*

PREP: 10 MIN. • **BAKE:** 20 MIN. + COOLING • **MAKES:** 2 DOZEN

1 pkg. (16½ oz.) refrigerated chocolate chip cookie dough
2 cups chocolate-covered peanuts
1 cup miniature marshmallows
½ cup butterscotch ice cream topping

1. Press cookie dough into an ungreased 13x9-in. baking pan. Bake at 350° for 14-16 minutes or until edges are lightly browned and center is set. Sprinkle with peanuts and marshmallows; drizzle with ice cream topping.

2. Bake 6-8 minutes longer or until marshmallows are puffed. Cool completely and cut into bars.

1 BAR: 175 cal., 8g fat (3g sat. fat), 6mg chol., 71mg sod., 24g carb. (6g sugars, 1g fiber), 3g pro. **DIABETIC EXCHANGES:** 2 fat, 1 starch.

Valentine Cutouts

Cool, fruity and creamy, these gelatin treats are richer than plain gelatin and cut easily into whatever shape you'd like. They're a fun finger food that works for any holiday or theme.
—*Annette Ellyson, Carolina, WV*

PREP: 45 MIN. + CHILLING • **MAKES:** 2 DOZEN

2 pkg. (6 oz. each) cherry or raspberry gelatin
2½ cups boiling water
1 cup cold milk
1 pkg. (3.4 oz.) instant vanilla pudding mix

1. In a bowl, dissolve gelatin in water; set aside for 30 minutes. In a small bowl, whisk milk and pudding mix until smooth, about 1 minute. Quickly pour into gelatin; whisk until well blended. Pour into an oiled 13x9-in. dish. Chill until set. Cut into cubes or cut using a heart-shaped cookie cutter.

1 PIECE: 73 cal., 0 fat (0 sat. fat), 1mg chol., 62mg sod., 16g carb. (16g sugars, 0 fiber), 2g pro.

Peanut Butter Cutout Cookies

I used peanut butter in place of the butter in my take on a traditional cutout cookie, which turned out super nutty and soft. My kids love to decorate them with frosting and sprinkles.
—*Cindi Bauer, Marshfield, WI*

PREP: 30 MIN. + CHILLING • **BAKE:** 10 MIN./BATCH + COOLING • **MAKES:** ABOUT 4½ DOZEN

1 cup creamy
  peanut butter
¾ cup sugar
¾ cup packed
  brown sugar
2 large eggs,
  room temperature
⅓ cup 2% milk
1 tsp. vanilla extract
2½ cups all-purpose flour
½ tsp. baking powder
½ tsp. baking soda
  Vanilla frosting
  Red food coloring
  Assorted colored
  sprinkles

1. In a large bowl, cream peanut butter and sugars until light and fluffy, about 4 minutes. Beat in eggs, milk and vanilla. Combine the flour, baking powder and baking soda; add to creamed mixture and mix well. Cover and refrigerate for 2 hours or until easy to handle.

2. On a lightly floured surface, roll out dough to ¼-in. thickness. Cut with 2-in. to 4-in. cookie cutters. Place 2 in. apart on ungreased baking sheets.

3. Bake at 375° for 7-9 minutes or until edges are browned. Cool for 1 minute before removing from pans to wire racks to cool completely. Frost cookies and decorate as desired.

2 EACH: 151 cal., 5g fat (1g sat. fat), 16mg chol., 84mg sod., 22g carb. (12g sugars, 1g fiber), 4g pro.

READER REVIEW
"I love this recipe! The peanut butter flavor is very subtle, so it still tastes very much like sugar cookies should…just with a wonderful twist!"
—BIKENVIKEN, TASTEOFHOME.COM

Homemade Strawberry Ice Cream

Who cares if it's cold outside in February? This creamy, luscious ice cream will remind you of the signature summer treat served at drive-in restaurants and ice cream socials. What dessert could be better?
—*Esther Johnson, Merrill, WI*

PREP: 20 MIN. + COOLING • **PROCESS:** 20 MIN./BATCH + FREEZING
MAKES: 12 SERVINGS (ABOUT 1½ QT.)

- 6 **large egg yolks**
- 2 **cups whole milk**
- 1 **cup sugar**
- ¼ **tsp. salt**
- 1 **tsp. vanilla extract**
- 2 **cups heavy whipping cream**
- 2 **cups crushed fresh strawberries, sweetened**

1. Place the egg yolks and milk in the top of a double boiler; beat. Add sugar and salt. Cook over simmering water, stirring until mixture is thickened and coats a metal spoon. Cool.

2. Add the vanilla, cream and strawberries. Pour into the cylinder of an ice cream freezer and freeze according to the manufacturer's directions. When ice cream is frozen, transfer to a freezer container; freeze for 2-4 hours before serving.

½ CUP: 265 cal., 19g fat (11g sat. fat), 166mg chol., 88mg sod., 22g carb. (21g sugars, 1g fiber), 4g pro.

Toppings add texture and flavor to scoops of ice cream. Whether you opt for just a couple or a dozen, there's no such thing as too many!

Nuts: peanuts, almonds, cashews, pecans, walnuts

Fruit: blueberries, raspberries, blackberries, strawberries, bananas, kiwis, pears, pineapple

Sweets: candies, crushed cookies, chocolate chips, butterscotch chips, granola, marshmallows, graham cracker crumbs, brownie bits

Salty and Savory: instant coffee grounds, bacon crumbles, potato chips

The Grand Finale: whipped cream, rainbow sprinkles, maraschino cherries

Valentine Heart Brownies

Steal hearts this Valentine's Day with brownies that have cute, yummy frosting centers. The treats have a subtle mint flavor that's simply irresistible!
—Taste of Home *Test Kitchen*

PREP: 35 MIN. • BAKE: 20 MIN. + COOLING • MAKES: 15 SERVINGS

1 **pkg. fudge brownie mix (13x9-in. pan size)**
¼ **tsp. mint extract**
½ **cup butter, softened**
1½ **cups confectioners' sugar**
¼ **tsp. vanilla extract**
Red paste food coloring, optional
¼ **cup baking cocoa**

1. Prepare brownie mix according to package directions, adding mint extract to batter. Transfer to a greased 13x9-in. baking pan. Bake at 350° for 20-25 minutes or until a toothpick inserted in the center comes out clean. Cool completely on a wire rack.

2. Meanwhile, in a bowl, cream the butter, confectioners' sugar, vanilla and, if desired, food coloring until light and fluffy. Transfer to a pastry bag. Set aside.

3. Line a baking sheet with parchment. Dust with cocoa; set aside. Cut brownies into 15 rectangles. Using a 1½-in. heart-shaped cookie cutter, cut out a heart from the center of each brownie. Reserve cutout centers for another use. Place brownies on prepared baking sheet. Pipe frosting into centers of brownies.

1 BROWNIE: 334 cal., 18g fat (6g sat. fat), 42mg chol., 201mg sod., 41g carb. (30g sugars, 1g fiber), 3g pro.

Linzer Heart Cookies

This specialty cookie takes a little extra effort, but the delectable results are worth it.
I bake the tender jam-filled hearts when I need something fancy for special occasions.
—*Jane Pearcy, Verona, WI*

PREP: 20 MIN. + CHILLING • **BAKE:** 10 MIN./BATCH • **MAKES:** 3 DOZEN

1¼ cups butter, softened
1 cup sugar
2 large eggs, room
  temperature
3 cups all-purpose flour
1 Tbsp. baking cocoa
½ tsp. salt
¼ tsp. ground cinnamon
¼ tsp. ground nutmeg
⅛ tsp. ground cloves
2 cups ground almonds
  Raspberry jam
  Confectioners' sugar

1. In a large bowl, cream butter and sugar until light and fluffy. Add eggs, 1 at a time, beating well after each addition. Combine flour, cocoa, salt, cinnamon, nutmeg and cloves; gradually add to the creamed mixture and mix well. Stir in almonds. Refrigerate for 1 hour or until easy to handle.

2. On a lightly floured surface, roll out dough to ⅛-in. thickness. Cut with a 3-in. heart-shaped cookie cutter. From the center of half the cookies, cut out a 1½-in. heart or round shape.

3. Place on ungreased baking sheets. Bake at 350° for 10-12 minutes or until edges are golden brown. Remove to wire racks to cool.

4. Spread ½ tsp. jam over the bottom of the solid cookies. Sprinkle cutout cookies with confectioners' sugar; carefully place over jam.

1 COOKIE: 163 cal., 9g fat (4g sat. fat), 29mg chol., 101mg sod., 18g carb. (9g sugars, 1g fiber), 3g pro.

READER REVIEW
"It does take some effort to make these cookies, but they come out beautifully! This is actually the first cutout cookie recipe I have gotten to work. They are as pretty as the picture. The flavor reminds me a little of a gingerbread man, but with raspberry jam. They will be a new Valentine's Day tradition."
—ALLABOUTCOOKIES86, TASTEOFHOME.COM

Freezer Strawberry Shortbread Dessert

When I'm planning party menus, I include a few recipes I can make in advance. Here's a dessert I can make and freeze for up to two weeks before serving. A refreshing slice is always welcome after a big meal.
—*Cassie Alexander, Muncie, IN*

PREP: 25 MIN. + FREEZING • **MAKES:** 15 SERVINGS

1¼ cups crushed pretzels
¼ cup sugar
½ cup butter, melted

FILLING
1 can (14 oz.) sweetened condensed milk
½ cup nonalcoholic strawberry daiquiri mix, thawed
1 pkg. (8 oz.) cream cheese, softened
1 container (16 oz.) frozen sweetened sliced strawberries, thawed
1 carton (8 oz.) frozen whipped topping, thawed

SAUCE
1 container (16 oz.) frozen sweetened sliced strawberries, thawed and undrained

1. In a small bowl, combine the pretzels, sugar and butter. Press mixture onto the bottom of a greased 11x7-in. dish. Refrigerate for 30 minutes.

2. For filling, in a large bowl, combine milk and daiquiri mix. Beat in the cream cheese until smooth. Stir in the strawberries; fold in whipped topping. Pour over crust (dish will be full). Freeze for 4 hours before serving.

3. For sauce, puree thawed undrained strawberries in a food processor or blender. Strain through a fine sieve. Drizzle over top.

1 PIECE: 349 cal., 17g fat (11g sat. fat), 41mg chol., 240mg sod., 48g carb. (40g sugars, 1g fiber), 4g pro.

NOTES

Chocolate Chip Red Velvet Whoopie Pies

Baking a fun treat is a must when my four grandchildren come for "Grandma Camp." This year I'll recruit the oldest, Henry, to help pipe the cake batter.
—*Linda Schend, Kenosha, WI*

PREP: 45 MIN. + CHILLING • **BAKE:** 10 MIN./BATCH + COOLING • **MAKES:** 2 DOZEN

1 pkg. red velvet cake mix (regular size)
3 large eggs, room temperature
½ cup canola oil
2 tsp. vanilla extract

FILLING
8 oz. cream cheese, softened
½ cup butter, softened
2 cups confectioners' sugar
1 cup miniature semisweet chocolate chips

1. Preheat oven to 350°. In a large bowl, combine cake mix, eggs, oil and extract; beat on low speed 30 seconds. Beat on medium 2 minutes.

2. Transfer batter to pastry bag; cut a ½-in. hole in the tip of bag. Pipe 1½x1-in. hearts onto parchment-lined baking sheets, spacing hearts 1 in. apart.

3. Bake until edges are set, 6-8 minutes. Cool on pans 2 minutes. Remove to wire racks to cool completely.

4. For filling, in a large bowl, beat cream cheese and butter until blended. Gradually beat in confectioners' sugar until smooth. Stir in chocolate chips. Spread filling on bottoms of half of the cookies. Top with the remaining cookies. Refrigerate leftovers.

1 WHOOPIE PIE: 267 cal., 16g fat (6g sat. fat), 44mg chol., 194mg sod., 30g carb. (23g sugars, 1g fiber), 2g pro.

Strawberry Cupcakes with Whipped Cream Frosting

Fresh strawberries are full of water, so they have a tendency to weigh down cake batters and make soggy cakes. That's why these strawberry cupcakes rely on strawberry jam or preserves. The concentrated flavor is just right for light and tender cupcakes.
—*Lisa Kaminski, Wauwatosa, WI*

PREP: 20 MIN. • **BAKE:** 20 MIN. + COOLING • **MAKES:** 16 CUPCAKES

½ cup seedless strawberry jam or preserves, warmed
¾ cup butter, softened
1 cup sugar
3 large egg whites, room temperature
1 tsp. vanilla extract
1 cup 2% milk
½ cup sour cream
1⅔ cups all-purpose flour
1 tsp. baking powder
¼ tsp. baking soda
¼ tsp. salt
Red food coloring, optional

FROSTING
2 cups heavy whipping cream
⅓ cup confectioners' sugar
⅓ cup seedless strawberry jam or preserves
½ tsp. vanilla extract
Fresh strawberries, optional

1. Preheat oven to 350°. Line 16 muffin cups with paper or foil liners. Press warm jam through a fine-mesh strainer. Discard pulp.

2. In a large bowl, cream butter and sugar until light and fluffy, 5-7 minutes. Add egg whites, 1 at a time, beating well after each addition. Beat in strained jam and vanilla. In a small bowl, whisk milk and sour cream until smooth. In another bowl, whisk flour, baking powder, baking soda and salt; add to the creamed mixture alternately with milk mixture, beating well after each addition. If desired, stir in food coloring.

3. Fill prepared muffin cups three-fourths full. Bake until a toothpick inserted in the center comes out clean, 20-25 minutes. Cool 10 minutes before removing to wire racks to cool completely.

4. In a large bowl, beat cream until it begins to thicken. Add confectioners' sugar, jam and vanilla; beat until stiff peaks form. Spread or pipe over cupcakes. Refrigerate leftovers. If desired, garnish with fresh strawberries.

1 CUPCAKE: 353 cal., 21g fat (13g sat. fat), 60mg chol., 184mg sod., 38g carb. (27g sugars, 0 fiber), 4g pro.

CHAPTER 9
All You Need Is Love...and Chocolate

Tuxedo Strawberries

These chocolate-dipped strawberries are surprisingly easy to decorate and are guaranteed to elicit oohs and aahs from all the pretty ladies and dapper dudes.
—*Gisella Sellers, Seminole, FL*

PREP: 1 HOUR + CHILLING • MAKES: 1½ DOZEN

18 medium fresh
  strawberries
  with stems
1 cup vanilla or
  white chips
3½ tsp. shortening, divided
1⅓ cups semisweet
  chocolate chips

NOTES

_____
_____
_____
_____
_____
_____
_____
_____
_____
_____

1. Line a tray or baking sheet with waxed paper; set aside. Wash strawberries and pat until completely dry.

2. In a microwave-safe bowl, melt the vanilla chips and 1½ tsp. shortening at 70% power; stir until smooth. Dip each strawberry until two-thirds is coated, forming the tuxedo shirt, allowing any excess to drip off. Place on prepared tray; chill for 30 minutes or until set.

3. Melt the chocolate chips and remaining shortening. To form the tuxedo jacket, dip each side of berry into chocolate from the tip of the strawberry to the top of vanilla coating. Repeat on the other side, leaving a white V-shape in the center. Set remaining chocolate aside. Chill berries for 30 minutes or until set.

4. Remelt remaining chocolate if necessary. Using melted chocolate and a round #2 pastry tip, pipe a bow tie at the top of the white V and 3 buttons down front of shirt. Chill for 30 minutes or until set. Store in the refrigerator in a covered container for up to 1 day.

1 STRAWBERRY: 121 cal., 8g fat (4g sat. fat), 1mg chol., 10mg sod., 14g carb. (13g sugars, 1g fiber), 1g pro.

Truffle Topiary

I wanted to give family and friends a treat they'd remember, so I whipped up batches of these multi-flavored truffles. Serve them as part of a cookie or candy platter or turn them into a stunning topiary centerpiece.
—Elisa Schmidt, Bethel Park, PA

PREP: 1 HOUR + STANDING • **COOK:** 15 MIN. + CHILLING • **MAKES:** 11 DOZEN

3 pkg. (12 oz. each) semisweet chocolate chips, divided
2¼ cups sweetened condensed milk, divided
½ tsp. orange extract
½ to 1 tsp. peppermint extract
½ tsp. almond extract
¾ lb. white candy coating, coarsely chopped
¾ lb. dark chocolate candy coating, coarsely chopped
½ cup ground almonds
1 each 6- and 8-in. Styrofoam cones or a single 12-in. cone

1. In a microwave-safe bowl, melt 1 package semisweet chocolate chips. Add ¾ cup condensed milk; mix well. Stir in orange extract. Cover and chill until firm enough to shape, about 45 minutes. Repeat 2 more times with remaining chips and milk, adding peppermint extract to 1 portion and almond extract to the other.

2. To make the truffles, shape chilled mixture into 1-in. balls; place on 3 separate waxed paper-lined baking sheets. Chill 1-2 hours or until firm.

3. Melt white candy coating in a microwave-safe bowl. Dip orange-flavored balls in coating and return to the waxed paper to harden. Melt remaining white candy coating again and dip balls once more to thoroughly cover. Let harden.

4. Melt chocolate candy coating in a microwave-safe bowl. Dip peppermint-flavored balls in coating and return to the waxed paper to harden.

5. Roll the almond-flavored truffles in ground almonds.

6. To make the tree, brush the Styrofoam cones with the remaining chocolate if desired. Using toothpicks, stick 1 end into each truffle and the other end into the cone, covering entire cone with truffles.

1 TRUFFLE: 83 cal., 4g fat (3g sat. fat), 2mg chol., 7mg sod., 11g carb. (10g sugars, 1g fiber), 1g pro.

Chocolate Marshmallow Cutouts

I make rich, fudgy cookies that taste like brownies with a marshmallow filling. I usually use heart-shaped cutters, but I've also left them uncut and filled with pink marshmallow creme.
—*Kelly Ward, Stratford, ON*

PREP: 35 MIN. + CHILLING • **BAKE:** 10 MIN./BATCH + COOLING • **MAKES:** ABOUT 2 DOZEN

1¼ **cups butter, softened**
2 **cups sugar**
2 **large eggs, room temperature**
2 **tsp. vanilla extract**
2 **cups all-purpose flour**
¾ **cup baking cocoa**
1 **tsp. baking soda**
½ **tsp. salt**
1 **jar (7 oz.) marshmallow creme**

1. In a large bowl, cream butter and sugar until light and fluffy. Beat in eggs and vanilla. In another bowl, whisk flour, cocoa, baking soda and salt; gradually beat into creamed mixture. Refrigerate, covered, 1 hour or until firm enough to shape.

2. Preheat oven to 350°. Shape level tablespoon of dough into balls; place 2 in. apart on ungreased baking sheets. Bake until the cookies are set, 6-8 minutes. Using a 1¼-in. heart-shaped cookie cutter, score the center of half of the cookies. Cool completely on pans on wire racks.

3. Using the same heart-shaped cookie cutter, gently cut scored cookie tops and remove the center of each. Spread marshmallow creme over the bottom of the solid cookies; cover with remaining cookies.

FREEZE OPTION: Freeze shaped balls of dough on baking sheets until firm. Transfer to an airtight freezer container; return to freezer. To use, bake cookies as directed.

1 SANDWICH COOKIE: 197 cal., 9g fat (5g sat. fat), 35mg chol., 164mg sod., 28g carb. (19g sugars, 1g fiber), 2g pro.

Chocolate Lover's Pizza

I created this after my dad said that my graham cracker crust should be topped with dark chocolate and pecans. It's easy to customize by adding your favorite chocolate and toppers. Dad thinks the whole world should know about this pizza!
—*Kathy Rairigh, Milford, IN*

PREP: 10 MIN. • **BAKE:** 10 MIN. + CHILLING • **MAKES:** 16 SLICES

2½ cups graham cracker crumbs
⅔ cup butter, melted
½ cup sugar
2 pkg. Dove dark chocolate candies (9½ oz. each)
½ cup chopped pecans

1. Combine the cracker crumbs, butter and sugar; press onto a greased 12-in. pizza pan.

2. Bake at 375° for 7-9 minutes or until lightly browned. Top with chocolate candies; bake for 2-3 minutes longer or until chocolate is softened.

3. Spread chocolate over crust; sprinkle with nuts. Cool on a wire rack for 15 minutes. Refrigerate for 1-2 hours or until set.

1 SLICE: 349 cal., 23g fat (12g sat. fat), 24mg chol., 133mg sod., 37g carb. (26g sugars, 3g fiber), 3g pro.

Chocolate Swirl Delight

I made a few alterations to a great recipe and ended up with an impressive dessert. Everyone loves its light texture and chocolaty flavor.
—*Lynne Bargar, Saegertown, PA*

PREP: 25 MIN. + CHILLING • **MAKES:** 12 SERVINGS

1½ pkg. (13 oz. each) Swiss cake rolls
2¾ cups 2% milk
2 pkg. (3.9 oz. each) instant chocolate fudge pudding mix
2 cups whipped topping

1. Cut each cake roll into 6 slices; reserve any broken chocolate coating for topping. Line bottom and sides of a 9-in. springform pan with cake slices, covering completely.

2. Whisk milk and pudding mixes 2 minutes (mixture will be thick); spread onto bottom layer of cake rolls. Cover with whipped topping. Sprinkle with reserved chocolate pieces. Refrigerate, covered, at least 2 hours before serving.

1 SLICE: 331 cal., 12g fat (5g sat. fat), 16mg chol., 382mg sod., 46g carb. (35g sugars, 1g fiber), 4g pro.

All Coupled Up

Play Cupid with your sips and sweets by trying these perfect-match wine pairings.

MOSCATO D'ASTI Light and sweet, with a hint of bubbles and a slight orange flavor. Pairs well with white chocolate, orange-flavored chocolate, orange candy or kumquats dipped in semisweet chocolate.

CRANBERRY WINE Both sweet and tart with intense cranberry flavor. This pairs well with rich, buttery dark chocolate truffles (the darker the better).

BRACHETTO D'ACQUI This chocolate pairing all-star is slightly sweet and effervescent, with strawberry and red fruit flavors. Pairs well with sampler of assorted chocolates; strawberries dipped in chocolate.

ASTI SPUMANTE Sweet and sparkling, with aromas of flowers and ripe summer fruits. Pairs well with dried apricots or pretzels dipped in bittersweet chocolate; sea foam candy.

TAWNY PORT Caramelly and nutty with hints of cinnamon and clove. Pairs well with chocolate hazelnut truffles, chocolate cashew clusters, chocolate cheese (from the cheese case).

Art with Heart

Gather used wine corks (try those from both red and white wines to get this ombre effect) and place them side by side, top side down, in an empty heart-shaped box until the box is filled.

DIY Wine Labels

Cut scrapbook paper so it's wide enough to cover the existing wine label and long enough to wrap around each bottle. Write the names of the wines on the strips of paper, then wrap around bottles and secure at the back with tape.

Chocolate-Covered Strawberry Cobbler

I love chocolate-covered strawberries, so I decided to try a fun twist on those flavors in a cobbler. Top it with whipped cream, either plain or with a little chocolate syrup stirred in.
—*Andrea Bolden, Unionville, TN*

PREP: 15 MIN. • **BAKE:** 35 MIN. + STANDING • **MAKES:** 12 SERVINGS

1 cup butter, cubed
1½ cups self-rising flour
2¼ cups sugar, divided
¾ cup 2% milk
1 tsp. vanilla extract
⅓ cup baking cocoa
4 cups fresh strawberries, quartered
2 cups boiling water
Whipped cream and additional strawberries

1. Preheat oven to 350°. Place butter in a 13x9-in. baking pan; heat pan in oven 3-5 minutes or until butter is melted. Meanwhile, in a large bowl, combine flour, 1¼ cups sugar, milk and vanilla until well blended. In a small bowl, mix cocoa and remaining sugar.

2. Remove baking pan from oven; add batter. Sprinkle with strawberries and cocoa mixture; pour boiling water evenly over top (do not stir). Bake for 35-40 minutes or until a toothpick inserted into cake portion comes out clean. Let stand 10 minutes. Serve warm with whipped cream and additional strawberries.

1 SERVING: 368 cal., 16g fat (10g sat. fat), 42mg chol., 316mg sod., 55g carb. (41g sugars, 2g fiber), 3g pro.

Chocolate Pudding Pizza

My sister Brenda and I came up with this recipe while talking on the phone. My family loved the classic pairing of chocolate and peanut butter presented in a fun new way.
—*LaDonna Reed, Ponca City, OK*

PREP: 35 MIN. + CHILLING • **MAKES:** 12 SERVINGS

1 pkg. (17½ oz.) peanut butter cookie mix
1 carton (12 oz.) spreadable cream cheese, softened
1¾ cups cold milk
1 pkg. (3.9 oz.) instant chocolate pudding mix
1 carton (8 oz.) frozen whipped topping, thawed
¼ cup miniature semisweet chocolate chips

1. Preheat oven to 375°. Prepare the cookie mix dough according to package directions. Press into a greased 12-in. pizza pan. Bake until set, about 15 minutes; cool.

2. Beat cream cheese until smooth. Spread over crust. In another bowl, beat milk and pudding mix on medium speed for 2 minutes. Spread over cream cheese layer. Refrigerate until set, about 20 minutes. Spread with whipped topping. Sprinkle with chips. Chill for 1-2 hours.

1 SLICE: 449 cal., 26g fat (12g sat. fat), 37mg chol., 376mg sod., 46g carb. (13g sugars, 1g fiber), 7g pro.

READER REVIEW
"I used a chocolate chip cookie mix instead and drizzled chocolate syrup on top. It turned out great! Everybody loved it and was asking for the recipe."
—MELISSA.BRUNO, TASTEOFHOME.COM

Slow-Cooker Chocolate Pots de Creme

Lunch-on-the-go just got sweeter. Tuck jars of rich chocolate custard into lunch boxes on Valentine's Day...or any day! These are fun for romantic picnics, too.
—Nick Iverson, Denver, CO

PREP: 20 MIN. • **COOK:** 4 HOURS + CHILLING • **MAKES:** 8 SERVINGS

2 cups heavy whipping cream
8 oz. bittersweet chocolate, finely chopped
1 Tbsp. instant espresso powder
4 large egg yolks, room temperature
¼ cup sugar
¼ tsp. salt
1 Tbsp. vanilla extract
3 cups hot water
Optional: Whipped cream, grated chocolate and fresh raspberries

1. Place cream, chocolate and espresso in a microwave-safe bowl; microwave on high until chocolate is melted and cream is hot, 4 minutes. Whisk to combine.

2. In a large bowl, whisk egg yolks, sugar and salt until blended but not foamy. Slowly whisk in cream mixture; stir in extract.

3. Ladle egg mixture into eight 4-oz. jars. Center lids on jars and screw on bands until fingertip tight. Add hot water to a 7-qt. slow cooker; place jars in slow cooker. Cook, covered, on low until set, about 4 hours. Remove jars from slow cooker; cool on counter for 30 minutes. Refrigerate until cold, about 2 hours.

4. If desired, top with whipped cream, grated chocolate and raspberries.

1 SERVING: 424 cal., 34g fat (21g sat. fat), 160mg chol., 94mg sod., 13g carb. (11g sugars, 1g fiber), 5g pro.

Salted Dark Chocolate Tart

My grandpa always kept a bag of caramels in his truck and a few in his pocket. Whether we were camping or going to a movie, he shared them with me. Now I try to put caramel in as many desserts as possible, including this sweet and salty tart, in memory of him.
—*Leah Tackitt, Austin, TX*

PREP: 30 MIN. • COOK: 15 MIN. + CHILLING • MAKES: 16 SERVINGS

1½ cups Oreo
    cookie crumbs
⅓ cup butter, melted

CARAMEL
¾ cup sugar
3 Tbsp. water
⅓ cup heavy
    whipping cream
2 Tbsp. butter, cubed
    Dash salt

FILLING
4 cups dark
    chocolate chips
1¼ cups heavy
    whipping cream
1 tsp. vanilla extract
½ tsp. large-crystal
    sea salt

1. In a small bowl, combine cookie crumbs and butter; press onto the bottom and up the sides of a greased 9-in. fluted tart pan with a removable bottom. Cover crust and refrigerate for 30 minutes.

2. For caramel, in a small saucepan over medium heat, combine sugar and water. Cook, shaking pan occasionally, until the sugar is melted and the mixture is almost clear (do not boil).

3. Increase heat to medium high; bring to a boil, without stirring. Cover and boil for 2 minutes, tightly hold lid of pan down. Uncover; shake pan. Cook 1-2 minutes longer or until mixture is amber, shaking pan several times.

4. Remove from the heat; stir in whipping cream (mixture will bubble) until smooth. Stir in the butter (mixture will bubble) and salt until blended. Pour into crust; refrigerate for 15 minutes.

5. Place the chocolate in a large bowl. In a small saucepan, bring cream just to a boil. Pour over chocolate; whisk until smooth. Stir in vanilla. Let stand for 20 minutes.

6. Pour over caramel. Sprinkle with sea salt. Refrigerate for at least 3 hours. Remove from the refrigerator about 45 minutes before serving.

1 PIECE: 552 cal., 37g fat (21g sat. fat), 46mg chol., 200mg sod., 56g carb. (43g sugars, 1g fiber), 5g pro.

Dark Chocolate Panna Cotta

Here, rich dark chocolate is accented by the flavor of sweet, ripe berries. Everything about this dessert, from the pretty presentation to its silky smooth texture, is special.
—*Susan Asanovic, Wilton, CT*

PREP: 25 MIN. • **COOK:** 10 MIN. + CHILLING • **MAKES:** 8 SERVINGS

1   **can (14 oz.) whole-berry cranberry sauce**
5   **Tbsp. raspberry liqueur, divided**
1   **envelope unflavored gelatin**
1   **cup cold 2% milk**
4   **oz. 53% cacao dark baking chocolate, chopped**
1½ **cups heavy whipping cream**
½   **cup sugar**
⅛   **tsp. salt**
2   **tsp. vanilla extract**
    Optional: Fresh raspberries and mint leaves

1. Place cranberry sauce in a food processor; cover and process until pureed. Strain and discard the pulp. Stir in 3 Tbsp. liqueur; set aside.

2. In a small bowl, sprinkle gelatin over milk; let stand for 1 minute. Meanwhile, place the chocolate in another small bowl. In a small saucepan, bring cream, sugar and salt just to a boil. Pour over chocolate; whisk until smooth.

3. Stir a small amount of chocolate mixture into gelatin mixture until gelatin is completely dissolved. Stir in 1 cup cranberry puree and vanilla. Pour into eight 6-oz. custard cups. Cover and refrigerate for 8 hours or overnight.

4. In a small bowl, combine the remaining cranberry puree and liqueur; cover and refrigerate until serving.

5. Unmold onto serving plates. Serve with sauce and garnish with raspberries and mint if desired.

1 SERVING: 397 cal., 22g fat (14g sat. fat), 63mg chol., 81mg sod., 45g carb. (36g sugars, 2g fiber), 4g pro.

Chocolate Bread Pudding

Traditional bread pudding is divine, but this one is especially decadent because it's chocolate. It's a comforting dessert that is sure to keep you and your sweetie warm on Valentine's Day.
—*Mildred Sherrer, Fort Worth, TX*

PREP: 15 MIN. + STANDING • BAKE: 30 MIN. • MAKES: 2 SERVINGS

2 oz. semisweet chocolate
½ cup half-and-half cream
⅔ cup sugar
½ cup 2% milk
1 large egg
1 tsp. vanilla extract
¼ tsp. salt
4 slices day-old bread, crusts removed and cut into cubes (about 3 cups)
Optional toppings: Confectioners' sugar and whipped cream

1. In a small microwave-wave bowl, melt chocolate; stir until smooth.

2. Stir in cream; set aside.

3. In a large bowl, whisk the sugar, milk, egg, vanilla and salt. Stir in chocolate mixture. Add bread cubes and toss to coat. Let stand for 15 minutes.

4. Spoon into 2 greased 2-cup souffle dishes. Bake at 350° until a knife inserted in the center comes out clean, 30-35 minutes.

5. Sprinkle with confectioners' sugar and top with a dollop of whipped cream if desired.

1 SERVING: 622 cal., 17g fat (9g sat. fat), 145mg chol., 656mg sod., 105g carb. (79g sugars, 2g fiber), 12g pro.

NOTES

_____
_____
_____
_____
_____
_____
_____

Raspberry Coconut Balls

My family loves Hostess Zingers, especially the raspberry flavor coated with coconut, inspiring this treat to sell at school bake sales. We can make about four dozen in 30 minutes, and they sell out fast!
—*Pam Clark, Wheaton, IL*

PREP: 30 MIN. • MAKES: ABOUT 4 DOZEN

1   pkg. (12 oz.) vanilla
    wafers, crushed
3⅓ cups sweetened
    shredded coconut,
    divided
1   can (14 oz.) sweetened
    condensed milk
3   tsp. raspberry extract
1   tsp. rum extract
¼   cup pink sanding sugar

Mix wafer crumbs and 1⅓ cups coconut. Stir in milk and extracts. In a shallow bowl, combine sugar and remaining coconut. Shape dough into 1-in. balls; roll in coconut mixture. Refrigerate in airtight containers.

1 COOKIE: 93 cal., 4g fat (3g sat. fat), 4mg chol., 52mg sod., 13g carb. (11g sugars, 1g fiber), 1g pro.

NOTES

_____

_____

_____

_____

_____

_____

Homemade Peanut Butter Cups

I choose pretty mini muffin liners and colored sprinkles to coordinate with the holiday we're celebrating. These irresistible candies with gooey peanut butter centers let anyone be a candymaker.
—*LaVonne Hegland, St. Michael, MN*

PREP: 20 MIN. + CHILLING • **MAKES:** 3 DOZEN

1 cup creamy peanut butter, divided
½ cup confectioners' sugar
4½ tsp. butter, softened
½ tsp. salt
2 cups semisweet chocolate chips
4 milk chocolate candy bars (1.55 oz. each), coarsely chopped
Colored sprinkles, optional

1. Combine ½ cup peanut butter, confectioners' sugar, butter and salt until smooth.

2. In a microwave, melt chocolate chips, candy bars and remaining peanut butter; stir until smooth.

3. Drop teaspoons of chocolate mixture into paper-lined mini muffin cups. Drop a scant teaspoon of peanut butter mixture into each cup; top with another teaspoon of the chocolate mixture. If desired, decorate with sprinkles. Refrigerate until set. Store in an airtight container.

1 PIECE: 123 cal., 8g fat (4g sat. fat), 2mg chol., 76mg sod., 12g carb. (10g sugars, 1g fiber), 3g pro.

READER REVIEW
"These treats were so easy and delicious. The recipe is simple to follow and the peanut butter cups look professional. I made them for Valentines Day and my family keeps asking for them again!"
—LJRAND, TASTEOFHOME.COM

Cashew Clusters

I make these sweet-salty treats for bake sales at the local community college where I work. They are always the first to sell out.
—*Betsy Grantier, Charlottesville, VA*

PREP: 20 MIN. + STANDING • COOK: 5 MIN. • MAKES: ABOUT 6 DOZEN

1 lb. white candy coating, coarsely chopped
1 cup semisweet chocolate chips
4 oz. German sweet chocolate, chopped
⅓ cup milk chocolate chips
2 cups salted whole cashews (about 9 oz.)
2 cups salted cashew halves and pieces (about 9 oz.)

1. Place first 4 ingredients in a large microwave-safe bowl; microwave, covered, at 50% power until melted, 5-6 minutes, stirring every 30 seconds. Stir in cashews.

2. Drop mixture by tablespoonfuls onto waxed paper-lined pans; let stand until set. Store in an airtight container.

1 PIECE: 95 cal., 6g fat (3g sat. fat), 0 chol., 46mg sod., 8g carb. (7g sugars, 1 fiber), 1 pro.

Pink Ice

You'll want to make plenty of room on your Valentine's Day goodies tray for this minty bark candy. With crushed peppermints and a pretty pink color, the pieces are festive and fun.
—*Phyllis Scheuer, Wenona, IL*

PREP: 10 MIN. + COOLING • MAKES: 10 OZ.

10 oz. white candy coating, coarsely chopped
2 Tbsp. crushed peppermint candies (about 7 candies)
¼ tsp. peppermint extract
2 drops red food coloring

1. In a microwave, melt candy coating at 70% power for 1 minute; stir. Microwave in additional 10- to 20-second intervals, stirring until smooth.

2. Stir in the crushed candies, peppermint extract and food coloring. Spread onto waxed paper to cool completely. Break into small pieces; store in an airtight container.

1 OZ.: 312 cal., 16g fat (15g sat. fat), 0 chol., 1mg sod., 42g carb. (40g sugars, 0 fiber), 0 pro.

Quick & Easy Gumdrops

These homemade sweet gummy bites are softer than store-bought varieties.
Their pretty color makes them perfect for Valentine's Day!
—*Leah Rekau, Milwaukee, WI*

PREP: 25 MIN. + CHILLING • **MAKES:** 64 PIECES (1 LB.)

3   **envelopes unflavored gelatin**
½   **cup plus ¾ cup water, divided**
1½ **cups sugar**
¼   **to ½ tsp. raspberry extract**
    Red food coloring
    Additional sugar

1. In a small bowl, sprinkle gelatin over ½ cup water; let stand 5 minutes. In a small saucepan, bring sugar and remaining water to a boil over medium heat, stirring constantly. Add gelatin; reduce heat. Simmer 5 minutes, stirring frequently. Remove from heat; stir in extract and food coloring as desired.

2. Pour into a greased 8-in. square pan. Refrigerate, covered, 3 hours or until firm.

3. Loosen edges of candy from pan with a knife; turn onto a sugared work surface. Cut into 1-in. squares; roll in the sugar. Let stand, uncovered, at room temperature until all sides are dry, turning every hour, 3-4 hours. Store candies between layers of waxed paper in an airtight container in the refrigerator.

1 PIECE: 19 cal., 0 fat (0 sat. fat), 0 chol., 1mg sod., 5g carb. (5g sugars, 0 fiber), 0 pro.

Chocolate-Covered Pretzels

The recipe for these chocolate-covered pretzels came from my grandma who loves to make candy and treats for my students. I follow in her footsteps and make these for co-workers and family members.

—*Aimee Worth, Fair Oaks, CA*

PREP: 1 HOUR + CHILLING • MAKES: 20 PRETZELS

20 **medium pretzel twists (about 5 oz.)**
12 **oz. milk chocolate candy coating disks, melted**
  Colored sprinkles
12 **oz. white candy coating disks, melted**

1. Dip 10 pretzels in milk chocolate, allowing excess to drip off. Place on waxed paper. Decorate half the pretzels with sprinkles. Chill for 10 minutes or until set.

2. Dip the remaining 10 pretzels in white candy coating, allowing the excess to drip off. Place on waxed paper. Decorate half the pretzels with colored sprinkles. Chill for 10 minutes or until set.

3. Drizzle the plain white-coated pretzels with melted milk chocolate. Drizzle the plain milk chocolate-coated pretzels with melted white candy coating. Chill for 10 minutes or until set. Store in an airtight container.

1 PRETZEL: 207 cal., 10g fat (9g sat. fat), 1mg chol., 143mg sod., 28g carb. (23g sugars, 0 fiber), 1g pro.

READER REVIEW
"I used regular large twisted pretzels. I dipped them halfway for a nice salty hit on one side."
—DUBLINLAB, TASTEOFHOME.COM

Macadamia & Coconut Caramels

I collect cookbooks from all over the world, and I use them to create new and different recipes. These smooth caramels have a scrumptious macadamia-coconut flavor. Who wouldn't want a little taste of the islands in February?
—*Sharon Delaney-Chronis, South Milwaukee, WI*

PREP: 25 MIN. • **COOK:** 25 MIN. + CHILLING • **MAKES:** 64 PIECES (1½ LBS.)

1 tsp. plus ½ cup butter, divided
1 cup packed light brown sugar
½ cup light corn syrup
¼ tsp. cream of tartar
¾ cup sweetened condensed milk
½ cup sweetened shredded coconut
½ cup chopped macadamia nuts
½ tsp. vanilla extract

1. Line an 8-in. square baking dish with foil and grease the foil with 1 tsp. butter; set aside.

2. In a large heavy saucepan, combine the brown sugar, corn syrup, cream of tartar and remaining butter; bring to a boil over medium heat, stirring constantly. Remove from the heat; gradually stir in milk. Cook and stir over medium-low heat until a candy thermometer reads 244° (firm-ball stage).

3. Remove from the heat; stir in remaining ingredients. Pour into prepared dish. Refrigerate until set, at least 2 hours.

4. Using foil, lift candy out of dish. Gently peel off foil; cut caramel into 1-in. squares. Wrap individually in waxed paper; twist ends. Store in an airtight container.

1 PIECE: 56 cal., 3g fat (1g sat. fat), 5mg chol., 23mg sod., 8g carb. (6g sugars, 0 fiber), 0 pro.

Salted Peanut Rolls

A gift of homemade candy is always a hit with sweet tooths.
I dip these peanut rolls in chocolate, but they're yummy plain, too.
—*Elizabeth Hokanson, Arborg, MB*

PREP: 1 HOUR + FREEZING • **MAKES:** ABOUT 5 DOZEN

1 jar (7 oz.) marshmallow creme
2 to 2¼ cups confectioners' sugar, divided
1 pkg. (14 oz.) caramels
2 Tbsp. water
4 cups salted peanuts, chopped
2 cups semisweet chocolate chips
2 tsp. shortening

NOTES

_____

_____

_____

_____

_____

_____

_____

_____

_____

1. Line two 15x10x1-in. pans with waxed paper. In a bowl, beat marshmallow creme and 1 cup confectioners' sugar until blended. Knead in enough remaining confectioners' sugar until mixture is smooth and easy to handle.

2. Divide mixture into 4 portions. Roll each portion into ½-in.-thick logs. Cut crosswise into 1½-in. pieces; place on 1 prepared pan. Freeze until firm, about 15 minutes. Meanwhile, heat caramels and water over low heat until melted, stirring occasionally. Working with one-fourth of the logs at a time, dip in melted caramel; roll in peanuts. Place on remaining prepared pan. Repeat with remaining logs; freeze coated logs until set.

3. In top of a double boiler or a metal bowl over barely simmering water, melt chocolate chips and shortening; stir until smooth. Dip bottom of rolls into melted chocolate; allow the excess to drip off. Return rolls to prepared pans. Refrigerate until set. Store between layers of waxed paper in an airtight container at room temperature.

1 PIECE: 154 cal., 9g fat (3g sat. fat), 0 chol., 48mg sod., 18g carb. (15g sugars, 2g fiber), 3g pro.

Black Cherry Swirl Fudge

This colorful treat has always been a favorite with my nine kids, eight grandkids and my Bible study group. I even vary the soft-drink flavors to match other holidays during the year.
—*Pauletta Bushnell, Lebanon, OR*

PREP: 30 MIN. + CHILLING • **MAKES:** ABOUT 3 LBS. (117 PIECES)

1½ tsp. plus ¾ cup butter, divided
3 cups sugar
¾ cup heavy whipping cream
1 pkg. (10 to 12 oz.) vanilla or white chips
1 jar (7 oz.) marshmallow creme
2 envelopes unsweetened black cherry soft drink mix

1. Line a 13x9-in. pan with foil and grease the foil with 1½ tsp. butter; set aside. In a heavy saucepan, combine the sugar, cream and remaining butter. Bring to a boil over medium heat, stirring constantly. Cook and stir mixture for 4 minutes.

2. Remove the heat; stir in vanilla chips and marshmallow creme. Pour 1 cup into a bowl; set aside. Stir black cherry drink mix into the remaining marshmallow mixture. Pour into prepared pan. Spoon reserved marshmallow mixture over top; cut through mixture with a knife to swirl.

3. Refrigerate for 1 hour or until firm. Using foil, lift fudge out of pan. Discard foil; cut into 1-in. squares. Store in an airtight container in the refrigerator.

1 PIECE: 55 cal., 3g fat (2g sat. fat), 6mg chol., 14mg sod., 8g carb. (8g sugars, 0 fiber), 0 pro.

Black Bottom Brandy Bites

The idea for these bite-sized tarts started with miniature bottles of chocolate brandy.
I place chocolate in the bottom of each pastry cup for an extra dash of fabulous.
—*Arlene Erlbach, Morton Grove, IL*

PREP: 30 MIN. • BAKE: 10 MIN. + COOLING • MAKES: 2 DOZEN

2 **sheets refrigerated pie crust**
1½ **cups mascarpone cheese**
¾ **cup turbinado sugar or sugar, divided**
⅓ **cup brandy**
½ **tsp. ground ginger, divided**
½ **tsp. vanilla extract**
½ **cup miniature semisweet chocolate chips, divided**
1¼ **tsp. pumpkin pie spice**

1. Preheat oven to 425°. Remove pie crusts from the refrigerator and bring to room temperature.

2. Stir together mascarpone cheese and ½ cup sugar. Add brandy, ¼ tsp. ginger and vanilla; stir until well blended. Fold in ¼ cup chocolate chips; cover and refrigerate.

3. Combine the pumpkin pie spice, remaining sugar and remaining ginger until well blended. On a lightly floured surface, unroll crusts; sprinkle evenly with sugar mixture. Lightly roll to help sugar mixture adhere. Cut crusts into 24 circles with a 2½-in. biscuit or round cookie cutter; discard scraps. Lightly press circles, sugar side up, into 24 mini muffin cups coated with cooking spray. Pierce once with a fork.

4. Bake the cups until golden brown, about 10 minutes; remove from oven. Immediately sprinkle ¼ tsp. chocolate chips into each cup; spread to cover bottom. Cool cups in pan for 15 minutes before removing to a wire rack.

5. When cups are completely cool, place in refrigerator. Chill until chocolate is set, about 20 minutes. Spoon the brandy mixture into cups, or into a pastry bag fitted with a star tip and pipe mixture into cups. Sprinkle cups with remaining chocolate chips and, if desired, additional pie spice. Refrigerate, covered, until serving.

1 TARTLET: 244 cal., 18g fat (10g sat. fat), 38mg chol., 77mg sod., 17g carb. (9g sugars, 0 fiber), 3g pro.

Cotton Candy Champagne Cocktails

You'll love these whimsical champagne cocktails. The cotton candy melts away, leaving behind its pretty pink color.
—Taste of Home *Test Kitchen*

TAKES: 5 MIN. • **MAKES:** 6 SERVINGS

6 **Tbsp. raspberry-flavored vodka**
1 **bottle (750 ml) champagne, chilled**
1½ **cups pink cotton candy**

Add 1 Tbsp. vodka to each of 6 champagne flutes. Top with champagne; create a cotton candy garnish for each glass. To serve, stir in cotton candy.

1 COCKTAIL: 125 cal., 0 fat (0 sat. fat), 0 chol., 0 sod., 4g carb. (2g sugars, 0 fiber), 0 pro.

HOW TO PLAN A GALENTINE'S DAY PARTY
Make your girls feel special by throwing a Galentine's Day party that celebrates your cherished friendship.

ASSEMBLE THE SQUAD
Galentine's Day is a day to celebrate the girlfriends who make life wonderful, so be as inclusive as your budget allows. You could even ask each of your friends to invite a friend.

MASTER THE MENU
If you're hosting at home, consider the offerings in this book or ask each friend to bring along a dish to pass. You can include links to your favorite potluck recipes in the invitation.

TURN ON GREAT MUSIC
Make a playlist that includes classic, upbeat friendship-themed tunes like Cyndi Lauper's "Girls Just Want to Have Fun," Sister Sledge's "We Are Family" and Queen's "You're My Best Friend."

BREAK OUT THE CHOCOLATE
Girlfriends and chocolate go together like chocolate and, well, everything. Serve chocolate desserts or set out a bowl with Hershey's Hugs & Kisses.

GIVE OUT VALENTINES
Since Valentine's Day is right around the corner, give each of your ladies a handwritten note telling her why her friendship is meaningful to you.

PLAY GAL GAMES
Leslie Knope of *Parks and Recreation* includes storytelling as part of her Galentine's Day. You can do that. Or play slumber party-esque games such as "Never Have I Ever." Or organize a game of Pictionary or charades.

INSTAGRAM IT
Come up with an Instagram hashtag and notify your guests about it. Ask them to tag fun photos of themselves with friends, especially mutual friends. During the party, gather everyone around for a group selfie, and upload it to your Insta account with the hashtag.

Blackberry Daiquiri Sherbet

This summer I decided to try making sherbet, which is one of my favorites. Blackberries were in season in my mom's garden, and I love the flavor of daiquiris. Turns out the two blend together beautifully!
—*Shelly Bevington, Hermiston, OR*

PREP: 15 MIN. • **PROCESS:** 30 MIN. + FREEZING • **MAKES:** 1¼ QT.

3 cups fresh or frozen blackberries, thawed
1 cup sugar
¼ tsp. salt
1 can (12 oz.) evaporated milk
2 Tbsp. lime juice
1 tsp. rum extract
½ tsp. citric acid

1. Place blackberries, sugar and salt in a food processor; process until smooth. Press through a fine-mesh strainer into a bowl; discard seeds and pulp. Stir the remaining ingredients into puree.

2. Fill cylinder of ice cream maker no more than two-thirds full; freeze according to the manufacturer's directions. Transfer the sherbet to freezer containers, allowing headspace for expansion. Freeze until sherbet is firm, 8 hours or overnight.

½ CUP: 147 cal., 3g fat (2g sat. fat), 12mg chol., 96mg sod., 28g carb. (26g sugars, 2g fiber), 3g pro.

Honey Poppy Seed Fruit Salad

Though fresh fruit steals the show in this medley, the subtle honey sauce makes it an especially sweet treat. It takes just 10 minutes to assemble this easy salad, which tastes so good with brunch. If you don't have these particular fruits on hand, try blackberries, mangoes or peaches instead.
—*Dorothy Dinnean, Harrison, AR*

TAKES: 10 MIN. • **MAKES:** 8 SERVINGS

2 medium firm bananas, chopped
2 cups fresh blueberries
2 cups fresh raspberries
2 cups sliced fresh strawberries
5 Tbsp. honey
1 tsp. lemon juice
¾ tsp. poppy seeds

In a large bowl, combine the bananas and berries. In a small bowl, combine the honey, lemon juice and poppy seeds. Pour over fruit and toss to coat.

¾ CUP: 117 cal., 1g fat (0 sat. fat), 0 chol., 2mg sod., 30g carb. (23g sugars, 5g fiber), 1g pro.

I donut
know what i'd
do without you

Sugared Doughnut Holes

These tender, tasty doughnut bites are easy to make. Dress them in in a nice box and bowas a gift for a special someone.
—*Judy Jungwirth, Athol, SD*

TAKES: 20 MIN. • MAKES: ABOUT 3 DOZEN

1½ cups all-purpose flour
⅓ cup sugar
2 tsp. baking powder
½ tsp. salt
½ tsp. ground nutmeg
1 large egg, room temperature
½ cup 2% milk
2 Tbsp. butter, melted
Oil for deep-fat frying
Confectioners' sugar

1. In a large bowl, combine the flour, sugar, baking powder, salt and nutmeg. In a small bowl, combine the egg, milk and butter. Add to dry ingredients and mix well.

2. In an electric skillet or deep-fat fryer, heat oil to 375°. Drop dough by heaping teaspoonfuls, 5 or 6 at a time, into oil. Fry until browned, about 1-2 minutes, turning once. Drain on paper towels. Roll warm doughnut holes in confectioners' sugar.

1 DOUGHNUT HOLE: 47 cal., 2g fat (1g sat. fat), 7mg chol., 68mg sod., 6g carb. (2g sugars, 0 fiber), 1g pro.

Zippy Praline Bacon

We live on a lake and have many overnight guests, so I serve brunch often. I'm always looking for recipes to enhance the usual eggs and bacon. My husband came home from a men's brunch raving about this one, and the hostess shared the recipe. Just be sure to make more than you think you might need...everybody wants seconds.
—*Myrt Pfannkuche, Pell City, AL*

TAKES: 20 MIN. • MAKES: 20 PIECES

1 lb. bacon strips
3 Tbsp. brown sugar
1½ tsp. chili powder
¼ cup finely chopped pecans

1. Preheat oven to 425°. Arrange bacon in a single layer in 2 foil-lined 15x10x1-in. pans. Bake 10 minutes; carefully pour off drippings.

2. Mix brown sugar and chili powder; sprinkle over bacon. Sprinkle with chopped pecans. Bake until bacon is crisp, 5-10 minutes. Drain on paper towels.

1 SLICE: 58 cal., 4g fat (1g sat. fat), 8mg chol., 151mg sod., 2g carb. (2g sugars, 0 fiber), 3g pro.

Marbled Meringue Hearts

Pretty pastel cookies are a fun way to brighten any special occasion. Replace the vanilla with a different extract for a change of flavor.
—*Laurie Herr, Westford, VT*

PREP: 25 MIN. • **BAKE:** 20 MIN. + COOLING • **MAKES:** ABOUT 2 DOZEN

3 **large egg whites**
½ **tsp. vanilla extract**
¼ **tsp. cream of tartar**
¾ **cup sugar**
 Red food coloring

NOTES

_____
_____
_____
_____
_____
_____
_____
_____
_____
_____

1. Place the egg whites in a large bowl; let stand at room temperature for 30 minutes. Line baking sheets with parchment.

2. Preheat oven to 200°. Add vanilla and cream of tartar to egg whites; beat on medium speed until soft peaks form. Gradually beat in sugar, 1 Tbsp. at a time, on high until stiff peaks form. Remove ¼ cup and tint pink. Lightly swirl the pink mixture into remaining meringue. Fill a pastry bag with meringue. Pipe 2-in. heart shapes 2 in. apart onto prepared baking sheets.

3. Bake until set and dry, about 20 minutes. Turn oven off; leave meringues in oven until oven has completely cooled. Store in an airtight container.

1 MERINGUE: 27 cal., 0 fat (0 sat. fat), 0 chol., 7mg sod., 6g carb. (6g sugars, 0 fiber), 0 pro.

MERINGUE MAGIC
For the greatest volume, place egg whites in a clean metal or glass mixing bowl. Even a drop of fat from the egg yolk, or a film sometimes found on plastic bowls, will prevent egg whites from foaming. For this reason, be sure to use clean beaters.

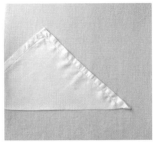

How to Make a Napkin Envelope

Give your table setting some love with this easy envelope napkin fold.

- Fold a napkin in half diagonally, with the point facing up. Then take the bottom corners and fold to meet in the middle.

- Fold the outer edges in once again so they meet in the middle.

- Fold the bottom half up and underneath, until it meets the base of the triangle.

- Fold down the triangle flap. Top with a meringue heart.

Buttermilk Pecan Waffles

Leslie Knope from *Parks and Recreation* includes waffles as part of her Galentine's Day celebration. We think she would approve of these nutty, golden waffles.
—*Edna Hoffman, Hebron, IN*

TAKES: 25 MIN. • **MAKES:** 7 WAFFLES (ABOUT 8 IN. EACH)

2 cups all-purpose flour
1 Tbsp. baking powder
1 tsp. baking soda
½ tsp. salt
2 cups buttermilk
4 large eggs, room temperature
½ cup butter, melted
3 Tbsp. chopped pecans

1. In a large bowl, whisk flour, baking powder, baking soda and salt. In another bowl, whisk buttermilk and eggs until blended. Add to the dry ingredients; stir mixture just until moistened. Stir in butter.

2. Pour about ¾ cup batter onto a lightly greased preheated waffle maker. Sprinkle with a few pecans. Bake according to manufacturer's directions until golden brown. Repeat with remaining batter and pecans.

1 WAFFLE: 337 cal., 19g fat (10g sat. fat), 159mg chol., 762mg sod., 31g carb. (4g sugars, 1g fiber), 10g pro.

Fresh Strawberry Syrup

One summer our garden yielded 80 quarts of strawberries! A good portion of that was preserved as strawberry syrup. We treat ourselves to this sweet, warm mixture over waffles or pancakes.
—*Heather Biedler, Martinsburg, WV*

TAKES: 15 MIN. • **MAKES:** 2 CUPS

¼ cup sugar
2 tsp. cornstarch
   Dash salt
2 cups chopped fresh strawberries
½ cup water
½ tsp. lemon juice

In a small saucepan, combine sugar, cornstarch and salt. Stir in strawberries, water and lemon juice until blended. Bring to a boil. Reduce heat; simmer, uncovered, until mixture thickens and berries are tender, 2-3 minutes.

¼ CUP: 40 cal., 0 fat (0 sat. fat), 0 chol., 19mg sod., 10g carb. (8g sugars, 1g fiber), 0 pro.

Sparkling Coconut Grape Juice

This sparkling drink is a nice change of pace from lemonade and party punch. The lime, coconut and grape combination is so refreshing. Add a splash of gin if you're feeling bold.
—*Shelly Bevington, Hermiston, OR*

TAKES: 5 MIN. • MAKES: 6 SERVINGS

4 **cups white grape juice**
2 **tsp. lime juice**
   Ice cubes
2 **cups coconut-flavored sparkling water, chilled**
   Lime wedges or slices

In a pitcher, combine grape juice and lime juice. Fill 6 tall glasses with ice. Pour juice mixture evenly into glasses; top off with sparkling water. Stir to combine; garnish with lime wedges, if desired.

1 CUP: 94 cal., 0 fat (0 sat. fat), 0 chol., 13mg sod., 24g carb. (21g sugars, 0 fiber), 0 pro.

Feta Asparagus Frittata

Asparagus and feta cheese come together to make this frittata extra special. Perfect for a lazy Sunday or to serve with a tossed salad for a light lunch.
—*Mildred Sherrer, Fort Worth, TX*

TAKES: 30 MIN. • MAKES: 2 SERVINGS

12 **fresh asparagus spears, trimmed**
6 **large eggs**
2 **Tbsp. heavy whipping cream**
   Dash salt
   Dash pepper
1 **Tbsp. olive oil**
2 **green onions, chopped**
1 **garlic clove, minced**
½ **cup crumbled feta cheese**

1. Preheat oven to 350°. Place ½ in. of water and the asparagus in a large skillet; bring to a boil. Cook, covered, until the asparagus is crisp-tender, 3-5 minutes; drain. Cool slightly.

2. In a bowl, whisk together eggs, cream, salt and pepper. Chop 2 asparagus spears. In an 8-in. cast-iron or other ovenproof skillet, heat oil over medium heat until hot. Saute green onions, garlic and chopped asparagus for 1 minute. Stir in egg mixture; cook, covered, over medium heat until eggs are nearly set, 3-5 minutes. Top with whole asparagus spears and cheese.

3. Bake until eggs are completely set, 7-9 minutes.

½ FRITTATA: 425 cal., 31g fat (12g sat. fat), 590mg chol., 1231mg sod., 8g carb. (3g sugars, 3g fiber), 27g pro.

Raspberry Meringue Hearts

Here's a lovely dessert your guests will think is almost too pretty to eat! I love the way the raspberry meringue easily drapes into a heart shape.

—*Mary Lou Wayman, Salt Lake City, UT*

PREP: 30 MIN. + STANDING • **BAKE:** 35 MIN. + COOLING • **MAKES:** 6 SERVINGS

3 **large egg whites**
¼ **tsp. cream of tartar**
   Dash salt
1 **cup sugar**
⅓ **cup finely chopped almonds, toasted**
1 **tsp. vanilla extract**

FILLING
3 **cups fresh or frozen unsweetened raspberries, thawed**
1 **tsp. cornstarch**
½ **cup seedless raspberry jam**
3 **cups raspberry or lemon sorbet**
⅓ **cup sliced almonds, toasted**
   Additional fresh raspberries, optional

1. Place egg whites in a small mixing bowl; let stand at room temperature for 30 minutes. Beat egg whites, cream of tartar and salt on medium speed until soft peaks form. Add sugar, 1 Tbsp. at a time, beating on high until stiff peaks form and sugar is dissolved. Fold in chopped almonds and vanilla.

2. Drop meringue into 6 mounds on a parchment-lined baking sheet. Shape into 4-in. hearts with the back of a spoon, building up the edges slightly. Bake at 300° for 35 minutes. Turn oven off; leave meringue in the oven for 1-1½ hours.

3. For filling, place the raspberries in a food processor. Cover and process until blended. Strain and discard seeds. In a small saucepan, combine the cornstarch, pureed raspberries and jam until smooth. Bring to a boil over medium heat, stirring constantly. Cook and stir for 1 minute or until thickened. Cool.

4. To serve, spoon sauce into meringue hearts. Place scoop of sorbet on top. Sprinkle with sliced almonds. Garnish with fresh raspberries if desired.

1 MERINGUE WITH ½ CUP SORBET AND ¼ CUP SAUCE:
423 cal., 7g fat (0 sat. fat), 0 chol., 53mg sod., 89g carb. (78g sugars, 6g fiber), 5g pro.

Raspberry Sour Cream Coffee Cake

Coffee and cake are like a wink and a smile. You'll take one without the other but given a choice, you want the pair. This fresh and fruity breakfast pastry is perfect for brunch. A drizzle of icing adds a nice finishing touch.
—*Debbie Johnson, Centertown, MO*

PREP: 20 MIN. • BAKE: 30 MIN. + COOLING • MAKES: 8 SERVINGS

1 cup fresh raspberries
3 Tbsp. brown sugar
1 cup all-purpose flour
⅓ cup sugar
½ tsp. baking powder
¼ tsp. baking soda
⅛ tsp. salt
1 large egg, room temperature
⅔ cup sour cream
3 Tbsp. butter, melted
1 tsp. vanilla extract
¼ cup sliced almonds

ICING
¼ cup confectioners' sugar
1½ tsp. 2% milk
¼ tsp. vanilla extract
Additional raspberries, optional

1. Preheat oven to 350°. In a small bowl, toss raspberries with brown sugar.

2. In a large bowl, whisk flour, sugar, baking powder, baking soda and salt. In another bowl, whisk egg, sour cream, melted butter and vanilla until blended. Add to flour mixture; stir just until moistened (batter will be thick).

3. Transfer half of the batter to a greased and floured 8-in. round baking pan. Top with raspberry mixture. Spoon remaining batter over raspberries; sprinkle with almonds.

4. Bake 30-35 minutes or until a toothpick inserted in center comes out clean. Cool in pan 10 minutes before removing to a wire rack to cool.

5. In a small bowl, mix confectioners' sugar, milk and vanilla until smooth; drizzle over top. Serve warm. If desired, serve with additional raspberries.

1 PIECE: 238 cal., 10g fat (5g sat. fat), 48mg chol., 154mg sod., 32g carb. (19g sugars, 2g fiber), 4g pro.

Amaretto Cherries with Dumplings

Treat everyone to a dessert of comfort food—warm tart cherries drizzled with amaretto and topped with fluffy dumplings. A scoop of vanilla ice cream is the perfect finishing touch.
—Taste of Home *Test Kitchen*

PREP: 15 MIN. • **COOK:** 7¾ HOURS • **MAKES:** 6 SERVINGS

2 cans (14½ oz. each) pitted tart cherries
¾ cup sugar
¼ cup cornstarch
⅛ tsp. salt
¼ cup amaretto or ½ tsp. almond extract

DUMPLINGS
1 cup all-purpose flour
¼ cup sugar
1 tsp. baking powder
½ tsp. grated lemon zest
⅛ tsp. salt
⅓ cup 2% milk
3 Tbsp. butter, melted
Vanilla ice cream, optional

1. Drain cherries, reserving ¼ cup juice. Place cherries in a 3-qt. slow cooker.

2. In a small bowl, mix sugar, cornstarch and salt; stir in reserved juice until smooth. Stir into cherries. Cook, covered, on high 7 hours. Drizzle amaretto or almond extract over cherry mixture.

3. For dumplings, in a small bowl, whisk flour, sugar, baking powder, lemon zest and salt. In another bowl, whisk milk and melted butter. Add to flour mixture; stir just until moistened.

4. Drop by tablespoonfuls on top of hot cherry mixture. Cook, covered, 45 minutes or until a toothpick inserted in center of dumplings comes out clean. If desired, serve warm with ice cream.

¾ CUP: 369 cal., 6g fat (4g sat. fat), 16mg chol., 242mg sod., 71g carb. (48g sugars, 2g fiber), 4g pro.

Recipe Index

E

Easy Glazed Bacon, 16
Easy Pink Lemonade Pie, 128
Elegant Smoked Salmon
  Strata, 10
English Marmalade Pecan
  Bread, 84

F

Favorite Coconut Cake, 131
Feta Asparagus Frittata, 198
Fluffy Cranberry Delight, 74
Freezer Strawberry
  Shortbread Dessert, 145
French Onion Soup with
  Swiss-Topped Toast, 56
Fresh Strawberry Syrup, 197

G

Garlic Clove Chicken, 109
Garlic Lemon Shrimp, 101
Glazed Doughnut Holes, 23
Gooey Chocolate-Peanut
  Bars, 134
Grilled Caprese
  Quesadillas, 47

H

Heart-Shaped Cinnamon
  Coffee Cakes, 79
Heart-Topped Chicken Potpie
  Soup, 57

Heart's Delight Eclair, 120
Heart's Desire Pizza, 97
Herb-Crusted Prime Rib, 105
Homemade Peanut Butter
  Cups, 172
Homemade Strawberry Ice
  Cream, 138
Honey Poppy Seed Fruit
  Salad, 190

L

Lemon Layer Cake, 124
Lemon Pound Cake
  Muffins, 91
Linzer Heart Cookies, 142
Lobster alla Diavola, 102

M

Macadamia & Coconut
  Caramels, 180
Mamaw Emily's Strawberry
  Cake, 119
Marbled Meringue
  Hearts, 194
Molded Strawberry Salad, 65
Mushroom & Spinach
  Saute, 74

O

One-Bowl Chocolate Chip
  Bread, 92
Oysters Rockefeller, 29

P

Parmesan Creamed
  Spinach, 66
Peanut Butter Cutout
  Cookies, 137
Peanut Butter, Strawberry &
  Honey Sandwich, 52
Pink Ice, 175

Q

Quick & Easy Gumdrops, 176
Quick Tomato Soup, 55

R

Raspberry Cake, 115
Raspberry Coconut Balls, 171
Raspberry Meringue
  Hearts, 201
Raspberry Pecan Chicken
  Salad, 48
Raspberry Sour Cream
  Coffee Cake, 202
Red Cabbage with Bacon, 77
Red Velvet Cinnamon
  Rolls, 83
Rhubarb Lemonade
  Slush, 40
Roasted Brussels Sprouts
  & Cauliflower, 70
Rosemary Strawberry
  Daiquiri, 26